The Colorado
Gardener's Companion

Gardener's Companion Series

The Colorado Gardener's Companion

*An Insider's Guide to Gardening
in the Centennial State*

Jodi Torpey

The
Globe
Pequot
Press

GUILFORD, CONNECTICUT

Copyright © 2007 by Morris Book Publishing, LLC

Text design by Casey Shain
Illustrations by Josh Yunger
Map by M. A. Dubé © Morris Book Publishing, LLC

Library of Congress Cataloging-in-Publication Data
Torpey, Jodi B., 1953–
   The Colorado gardener's companion : an insider's guide to gardening in the centennial state / Jodi Torpey. — 1st ed.
       p. cm. — (Gardener's companion series)
     Includes index.
     ISBN-13: 978-0-7627-4308-7
     ISBN-10: 0-7627-4308-5
   1. Gardening—Colorado. I. Title. II. Series.
     SB451.34.C6T67 2007
     635.09788—dc22

                                                        2006033099

Manufactured in the United States of America
First Edition/First Printing

*For Shirley Rae Pendleton—
my garden inspiration*

Contents

Introduction viii

Firm Foundations

1. Scratching the Surface on Soils 2

2. Colorado's Growing Challenges 17

3. Water 34

Green Things

4. Vegetable Gardening 1-2-3 50

5. Annuals 71

6. Perennials 85

7. Trees and Shrubs 99

8. Lawn 114

9. Invasive Plants 129

Garden Solutions

10. Coping with Pests and Diseases 146

11. Learning from Special Places 159

Glossary 165

Appendix: Resources for the Colorado Gardener 169

Index 175

Introduction

Every garden in every corner of our state is different, but they all have one thing in common: They're tended by Colorado gardeners. Gardeners here have to cope with the challenges of a semiarid climate and soil that is rocky, sandy, or made of clay. Some areas struggle with a lack of snow cover in the winter and intense sunshine in the summer. Drying winds desiccate plant roots. Extreme temperature fluctuations frustrate even the most steadfast gardener.

If you're new to Colorado, you might not see the pleasure of gardening here. If you've arrived from one of those places where every seed you planted flourished and you never had trouble growing tomatoes, you may already have thrown in the trowel. If you've been gardening here a while, with luck you've learned how to make the most of what we have.

Gardening in Colorado may seem like an extreme sport, but it has its advantages, too. Because of our low humidity, there are fewer insect pests and plant diseases. We can grow beautiful lawns, flowers, shrubs, and trees. We also get to garden in some of the most scenic areas of the country.

This book is designed to help you get more from your Colorado gardening experience. Over a dozen experts from around the state—most of them gardeners just like you—provide advice and information for both the novice and experienced gardener. You'll learn how to take advantage of gardening in our dry climate and ways for dealing with the challenges of our wild weather. Practical, down-to-earth tips are included for flower and vegetable gardening, planting trees, dealing with pests, and landscaping to conserve water. Specific plant recommendations, from annuals to native perennials, are included throughout the book.

It's my happy duty as a master gardener to direct you to the many excellent resources provided by Colorado State University's

Cooperative Extension county offices, fact sheets, hotlines, and Web sites. These state-specific resources, as well as many of my other favorite gardening references, are included throughout the book and in the appendix. These resources may be of help whenever you undertake a challenging garden project or find a garden issue that has you stumped.

Success as a Colorado gardener has to do with amending the soil, encouraging healthy roots and selecting the right plants. You'll notice these are recurring themes throughout the book. If you master these, you're well on your way to growing great gardens.

Someone once told me, "If you're not killing plants, you're not really gardening." I took that adage to heart. I've made plenty of mistakes while gardening along the Front Range, but I've done a few things right along the way. I had a vision for my landscape and worked hard to accomplish it, and today that vision is a reality. My hope is this book helps make your garden dreams come true, too.

Firm Foundations

Scratching the Surface on Soils

Several years ago I was driving through Wisconsin on a quick business trip. It was a clear day in early spring, and the trip from Madison to Plain was refreshing. The rolling hills were lush and green and dotted with charming dairy farms that captured my imagination. It was a relaxing drive until I passed through a small town called Black Earth. As I drove through this lush valley, I couldn't keep my eyes on the road. Mile after mile, field after field, the ground was the darkest, richest, most fertile soil I had ever seen.

My gardener's instincts nearly caused an accident as I fought the urge to slam on the brakes. I longed to stop and fill the rental car's trunk, backseat, and even my suitcase with handfuls of that exquisite soil. I forced myself to keep driving, but I couldn't help daydreaming about a garden made of that beautiful black earth. What wonderful vegetables I could grow. How easy gardening could be with flower beds of that luscious black earth.

There's no black earth in Colorado. There's some red earth. Some clay earth. Some sandy earth. But no black earth, unless we create it. That's what makes gardening in Colorado so much fun. This chapter gives the basic information you need to build a firm foundation for your garden. It explains a little about Colorado soils, describes soil amendments, and gives tips for using amendments effectively.

Colorado has three main geographic areas: the eastern plains, the mountains, and the Western Slope. The Continental Divide is the imaginary dividing line that separates Colorado's Western Slope and its Front Range. Soil types vary depending on altitude and location and range from coarse-textured sandy soil to fine-textured clayey soil. Most of the soil is highly alkaline and has little organic matter—less than 1 percent. In comparison, ideal soils can contain as much as 5 percent organic matter. In a semi-arid climate like ours, where we get an average of 17 inches of annual precipitation (in a very wet year), it's no wonder we lack good black earth. The more rainfall an area receives, the more vegetation it grows. When that vegetation decomposes it becomes organic matter that makes for richer soils.

In the most populous area of the state, along the Front Range, soils are clayey. But head out toward the eastern plains and the soil is decidedly sandy. In the Grand Valley the soil is a silty clay loam but turns sandy the farther west you go. Mountain "soil" is mostly decomposed granite, but there are areas with clay soil, too. In the southwestern part of the state, soils range from silty loam to clayey to solid shale or rock.

Ideal soil has what's referred to as good soil tilth—the actual physical aspects of the soil that support plant growth. The three elements that contribute to tilth are the texture or size of the soil particles, how well these pieces fit together, and the amount of organic material in the soil.

Heavy clay soils are made of small, closely knit particles that hold water, practically drowning plants. The looser particles in coarse sandy soils allow water and nutrients to drain so quickly plants can hardly get a good drink. The solution to both problems is the same: Add organic matter. Organic matter, like compost, allows for better air and water circulation for clay soils and improves the water-retaining capability of sandy soil.

Your Brown Thumb

If you're looking for the one nugget of information that's guaranteed to make a difference in your gardening life, here it is: *The majority of plant growing problems start with the soil.* To be a successful Colorado gardener, you don't need a green thumb as much as you need a brown one. That brown thumb shows you know what kind of soil you're working with and what you can do to improve it.

You can start by using your senses to tell if your soil has the basic characteristics of ideal soil. Is it dark in color? Does it smell earthy?

Next, determine the texture of your soil by getting your hands dirty. Does it feel gritty, smooth, or sticky?

Add a little water to see if you can roll the soil into a little ball.

- If you can't roll it into a little ball or the ball won't hold its shape, the soil texture is most likely sand or sandy loam. (Loam is a combination of different particle sizes.)

- If you can roll the soil into a little ball and then crumble it easily, the soil texture is probably a sandy or silty loam.

- If you can roll the soil into a little ball that can be dried and used to play marbles, you have a clayey soil.

Another test is to simply dig a hole in the ground and fill it

Soil Texture Experiment

For detailed instructions on how to measure your soil's texture, turn to Colorado State University Cooperative Extension fact sheet 7.723 (see the resources appendix at the back of the book). You'll need a newspaper, soil sample, a quart jar with lid, powdered dishwasher detergent, and a little bit of time. At the end of the experiment, you'll know how much clay, silt, fine sand, and coarse sand you have in your soil.

Preparation, Preparation, Preparation

Location, location, location is the mantra for real estate. For Curtis E. Swift, PhD, a Colorado State University extension agent based in Grand Junction, the key to good gardening is preparation, preparation, preparation. Gardeners often make two mistakes when preparing soil for gardening: not cultivating deeply enough and using the wrong organic matter. Here are Swift's tips for gardening in and around Grand Junction, where clay soil is a fact of life.

- Add 3 to 6 cubic yards of organic matter per 1,000-square-foot area.

- Use organic matter with a particle size of ¼ to ½ inch or larger.

- Work in a small amount of organic matter at a time, in layers.

- Work to a depth of 18 inches, if possible. You may need a plow or small tractor, but deep soil preparation helps roots grow deeper.

- Avoid peat moss as an amendment. Don't use cow manure, bull manure, or mushroom compost because of the high salt content.

- Use the results of a soil test to see if there's a need for potassium and phosphorus. Many areas in the state have adequate levels

with water. Does it drain quickly? If so, sandy soil is probably the culprit. Does the water turn to mud and just sit there? Then you probably have clayey soil.

If you're not confident you have the knack to distinguish what kind of soil you have, don't worry. You can learn this information and more with a simple soil test.

Soil Testing

I confess. I've never conducted a real soil test in my yard. As an experienced Colorado gardener, I knew by the light brown color and the gritty feel of the dirt that it was sandy soil. I didn't take time for a soil test because I knew the xeric plants I planned for my water-wise landscape would feel right at home in that lean, well-drained soil. I'd also read that adding too much organic material can change the character of xeric plants. However, soil testing would have been useful for my postage-stamp vegetable garden. Looking back on my early growing experiences, I now understand why my first corn crop produced the smallest ears I'd ever seen.

Gardeners who prefer to take their time and have their soil tested before they start planting could be buying a plant insurance policy. Soil tests help uncover problems related to pH, salts, and fertilizer needs. Gardeners who test their soil as a first step find the recommendations useful for amending, planting, and irrigating. This is especially true for those gardening on a new site.

Routine soil tests are inexpensive ($15 to $20) and are available from a variety of sources around the state, including Colorado State University's Soil, Water and Plant Testing Laboratory (970–491–5061; www.colostate.edu/Depts/SoilCrop/ service.html). Private analytical labs also conduct soil analyses for home owners for about $20. The CSU Cooperative Extension can provide a list of commonly used labs (see the Resources appendix). Labs based in Colorado are a good choice, because these will give results correlated for Colorado soils. Most standard tests measure texture, pH, soluble salts, organic matter, lime, and nutrients (nitrogen, phosphorus, potassium, zinc, iron, copper, and manganese).

Additional tests can be requested, such as lead testing on an older site. Do-it-yourself tests aren't recommended for our area because the results are based on soil pH. Most of the soil tests sold for home use perform best where the soils are acidic—something that's rare in Colorado's alkaline soil environment.

Measuring pH

Some gardeners think soil is just stuff that holds plants in place and not the source of plant nutrients. In fact, soil conditions, nutrient levels, and pH levels impact how well plants will do in your garden.

A soil's pH is one condition that affects plant growth. Soil pH indicates the acidity or alkalinity of soil on a scale from 1 to 14, with 7 being neutral.

Soils with pH values less than 7 are considered high-acid soils. Plants like azaleas, blueberries, and rhododendrons thrive in soils with a pH value of 5.0 to 5.5. Some ornamental plants, grasses, and vegetables prefer a less acidic soil, something with a pH value of 5.8 to 6.5. Soils with pH values greater than 7 are alkaline soils.

Matching the plants to their soil pH preferences is important because pH affects the availability of nutrients within the soil. If the pH is wrong for a plant, it will be lacking the nutrients it needs to become healthy and vibrant. Soil pH indicates soil nutrient availability. The three categories of nutrients for good plant growth are primary nutrients, secondary nutrients, and micronutrients.

Primary nutrients are often needed in fairly large quantities. The top three are familiar to gardeners: nitrogen, phosphorus, and potassium. Calcium, magnesium, and sulfur are secondary nutrients and are required in smaller quantities. Micronutrients, like zinc and manganese, are needed in extremely small amounts.

Plant growth is related to the nutrients available in the soil. For instance, tomatoes need high nitrogen levels, especially in mid- to late summer, to increase tomato yield and to control a disease known as early blight.

In soils with high pH, micronutrients like manganese become more available, which can practically poison plants. In soils with low pH levels, nutrients like calcium and phosphorus become less available. Most of the micronutrients become less available when the soil is above pH 6.5.

Most soils in Colorado are highly alkaline, with a pH of 7.0 to 7.8. Colorado soils are also naturally high in calcium, which ties up iron so it's not available to plants. That's why trees with high iron needs don't do well in our calcareous soils. Plants need iron to produce chlorophyll and healthy green leaves. Iron chlorosis is an iron deficiency that causes leaves to turn yellow and plants to become less vigorous.

Gardeners in other parts of the country have success adding sulfur to lower their soil's pH level. However, this tactic doesn't work here because of the high calcium levels known as free lime.

You can quickly test for free lime by placing a spoon-size sample of dry soil in a container and pouring a little vinegar on it. A bubbling mixture signals free lime. If there's no reaction, sulfur products may be used to help lower the pH a bit, but probably not enough to grow acid-loving azaleas.

Taking a Soil Sample

Soil samples can be taken at any time, although gardeners usually gather samples after moving into a newly built site, moving into a home site new to them, or whenever they've made significant changes to the soil.

Taking a soil sample isn't complicated, but for best results samples should be taken for each area of the yard where different soil amendments and fertilizers are used. For example, garden bed samples should be kept separate from lawn area samples.

The results you receive from the lab will provide recommendations for soil management and fertilizer needs. However, a soil test isn't the solution to every gardening problem. Soil tests can't make recommendations about watering too much or too little— or not at all. Soil testing won't solve pest problems, weed worries, or bad planting choices.

Fertilizer Fun

Fertilizers are a soil amendment with a guaranteed percentage of the nutrients that plants need: nitrogen (N) for strong stems and green leaves, phosphorus (P) for flowering, and potassium (K) for healthy roots and stems. Gardens need regular doses of fertilizer because, over time, the nutrients are used or washed away. Apply only as directed. An application of too much fertilizer can be as bad as not applying enough.

I learned that lesson the hard way. If a little chicken manure is good, a lot of chicken manure is a bad idea. It adds too much nitrogen to the soil all at once. That year I grew beautiful tomato plants, but only a few tomatoes.

The labels on fertilizer products indicate the ratio of nutrients. For example, a label of 10-10-10 means the fertilizer has 10

Fertilizer Facts

- Flower and vegetable gardens need both organic matter and fertilizer.

- Fertilizers can be inorganic or organic.

- Inorganic (chemical) fertilizers have a guaranteed amount of nutrients that can be matched to your yard or garden needs and work faster than organic fertilizers.

- The amount of fertilizer to add to garden soil depends on the nitrogen needs and the existing amount of organic matter.

- Some gardeners prefer to garden organically and don't use chemical fertilizers.

- Organic fertilizers are derived from natural sources and help build nutrients in the soil; these also guarantee certain amounts of nutrients but work more slowly than chemical fertilizers.

- Never use fresh manure on vegetable gardens because of the potential for food contamination. Wait until the fall to add it to garden soil so it has time to break down before the next planting season.

- Other kinds of plant food include slow-release fertilizers that are added to the soil and water-soluble fertilizers that feed plants when watered.

percent nitrogen, 10 percent phosphorus, and 10 percent potassium. Every ten pounds of that fertilizer puts one pound of each element in the soil. Here's where the results of your soil-testing efforts pay off—you can choose a fertilizer with the correct combination of nutrients to meet your soil's needs.

For example, soils in some parts of the state, like Mesa, Delta, and Montrose Counties, typically have high concentrations of phosphorus and potassium. Gardeners might not need to add these nutrients unless a soil test recommends it.

The First Amendment

If your soil is like most in Colorado, you'll need to get in the habit of adding organic matter each growing season. Amendments are materials that are added into the soil to improve it. There are three kinds of soil amendments: those that improve the chemistry of the soil, those that increase organic matter in the soil, and those that improve tilth and either water drainage or retention.

Compost increases the organic matter in the soil and also improves soil texture and structure. Mulch is not a soil amendment, although some mulch materials eventually do break down to enrich the soil.

As tempting as it might be to add a ton—literally—of organic soil amendment all at once, it's not a good idea. Because only small amounts of nutrients become available over time, modest amounts of organic matter are best added each growing season.

If your soil is composed of less than the ideal 5 percent organic matter, limit each application to a 1-inch layer before cultivating or about 3 cubic yards per 1,000-square-foot area for annual gardens each growing season. Be sure to rototill organic matter to a depth of 6 to 12 inches. Perennial plants, lawns, trees, and shrub areas can receive 6 cubic yards per 1,000-square-foot area.

The first amendment in soil preparation means you have the freedom to choose whatever amendment you'd like to use, within reason. Take into consideration your soil needs and what you'd like the amendment to do. Do you need it to decompose slowly or quickly? Do you need to change the soil's texture to retain water or make it more permeable? Keep in mind that soils in Colorado are prone to a higher salt content and a higher pH level, so you'll want to avoid amendments, like cow manure, that raise these levels.

If you have sandy soil like mine, you'll want an amendment that starts to make a difference quickly. Compost is a good choice because it changes the soil's texture so it can hold water and nutrients longer. If you have clay soil, amendments like wood chips or straw help increase water permeability.

Other soil amendments include well-aged manure (six months or older), biosolids from treated sewage (only use Grade 1), and grass clippings. Adding organic matter not only improves the soil's tilth but it also provides food to help feed good bugs.

Black Gold

One of my happiest moments as a gardener came the day I discovered an ancient bag of leaves I'd raked years ago and stashed from view. As I lifted the bag, the brittle plastic fell apart in shreds and my legs, ankles, and shoes were covered with black, crumbly compost teaming with little earthworms. I quickly transferred that compost to the vegetable garden, worms and all.

Nature created compost for me then, but now I don't leave it to chance. Instead I compost my leaves, twigs, and pesticide-free grass clippings with coffee grounds, banana peels, eggshells, and vegetable peelings. I also shred and toss in paper towel cores, lint, and paper egg cartons. Dog fur also makes a good additive.

All organic matter decomposes eventually, but composting accelerates the process. The secret to composting success is

The Dirt on Compost

Judy Elliott, education coordinator for Denver Urban Gardens (DUG), would never let a bag of leaves compost alone. For more than fifteen years she's taught gardeners how to become master composters. Her approach to composting is to create a compost pile that will give the end product a high level of soil wellness. "A compost pile needs the same things people need for healthy growth," she says. Here are her top tips:

1. Create a home for the compost that achieves the volume of approximately 1 square yard. The compost pile should be about 3 feet wide by 3 feet long by 3 feet deep. Height of the pile is crucial.

2. Make sure the pile has water to sustain it—not drenching wet nor too dry. Water the pile in a slow pattern around and in the different layers. Keep the compost the consistency of a wrung-out sponge. It should look like it glistens.

3. Exercise the compost pile by turning the pile once a week or once every two weeks to keep the oxygen circulating. Mix layers by pulling the outside to the middle and flipping the top to the bottom.

4. Chop material before adding it to the pile. When the particle size of the materials is decreased, the size of the compost area is increased. Use a lawn mower, chipper, or sharp shovel to break up material into 1- or 2-inch pieces. Chop leaves in a trash can with a weed whacker.

5. Provide a balanced diet. Compost is a mixture of higher carbon material with higher nitrogen material (25 to 30 parts carbon to 1 part nitrogen). Make piles with brown materials that have been accumulating for some time with green materials from the garden or kitchen. Use a variety of materials, but never compost meat, cheese, fat, or bones.

For more composting information, contact Denver Urban Gardens (DUG) at www.dug.org or (303) 292–9900.

balancing these four essential elements: nitrogen (green things) carbon (brown things), moisture, and oxygen. Bacteria, fungi, worms, and sow bugs help the decomposing process along.

You can use my technique of forgetful composting or you can start your own system with a compost bin or compost pile. Compost bins come in two basic varieties. Batch systems make one batch of compost at a time; continuous-flow systems let you continuously add material so there's no waiting between batches. Look for a bin that's easy to use and has the ability to retain heat and moisture in our dry climate.

You could also create an open pile in the corner of the yard using snow fence or wooden pallets to contain it. Just be sure to keep enough water in it. Strong winds can dry out the pile in a hurry.

Grab several handfuls of leaves from under a bush, add a few shovels of garden soil, and you're on your way. Alternate adding layers of shredded dry brown material with green matter and toss in a little soil for good measure. Keep it moist. When you see worms in the compost, you know you're doing a good job. Till the compost into your garden, dig it in around perennials, and use it to top-dress the lawn.

If you want to try composting and you live in Colorado's bear country, Judy Elliott of Denver Urban Gardens says it shouldn't be a problem if you use only nonfood items. However, the pile still needs to be turned on a regular basis. "Just throwing in leaves and grass clippings would lead to compaction and odors from anaerobic composting conditions. Not the best when we're dealing with large critters." She recommends indoor composting using red wiggler worms instead.

Cover Crops

Another way to increase the amount of organic matter in your soil is by planting cover crops. Usually fast-growing crops like winter rye and winter wheat are planted to prevent soil blowing or eroding away.

Cover crops are sown in the fall and tilled into the garden in the spring. This "green manure" is a natural soil builder and adds nitrogen to the soil. Common cover crops include winter rye, buckwheat, vetch, winter pea, alfalfa, and clover. It's important to remember to till the crop into the garden before it goes to seed.

Mulch More

Mulch can be any organic or inorganic material placed on top of the soil surface. Mulch is used to preserve moisture and prevent weeds. Mulch also needs to be added more than once. Each spring my car is one of the first in line at Denver's free Treecycle Mulch Giveaway and Leafdrop Compost sale. This program is a cooperative effort between Denver Recycles/Solid Waste Management and Denver Parks and Recreation. The mulch is made by grinding thousands of discarded Christmas trees collected in December and January. The compost is produced from leaves gathered during each fall's leaf drop collection program.

When I get my pine chips home, I shovel the mulch about 3 or 4 inches deep on my flower beds but keep it away from the stems of my shrubs and trunks of my trees. The chips go wherever I need to control weeds, retain soil moisture, protect plants from temperature extremes, improve water penetration, and just make the area look nicer.

Many Colorado communities offer a similar mulch giveaway in the spring. Check with your local recycling organization or waste management company for availability in your area. If this isn't an option, other good sources for chipper mulch are landscape companies and tree-shrub management companies.

Mulched Christmas trees make a good mulch, but you can also use dry, chemical-free grass clippings, leaves, pine needles, sawdust, straw, wood chips, and pea gravel. Some plants are picky and prefer one kind of mulch over another. For example, plants with low water needs often prefer pea gravel over bark mulch.

The crushed gravel won't decompose, allows water to percolate slowly down to the roots, and can encourage plant growth with warmer soil temperatures.

A Note about Compaction

One other soil management problem that deserves a mention is soil compaction. If the soil becomes too compacted by foot or equipment traffic, roots can't penetrate the soil layers for optimum growth. In addition, water has a tendency to run off compacted areas. To avoid this problem, don't walk on cultivated soil (especially when the soil is wet), limit equipment traffic in that area, and keep adding that good old organic matter.

Colorado's Growing Challenges

Christina MacLeod lives in rural Westcliffe and understands the challenges of trying to garden at 8,000 feet. "The short growing season makes it impossible for some plants to flower, produce seed, or produce fruit. Animal predators—such as chipmunks, rabbits, squirrels, mice, voles, deer, and elk—offer even greater challenges and require creativity in outsmarting them," she says.

MacLeod has tried to garden on her windswept high plains property since 2001. There's too much shade, too much sun, too much wind, or not enough moisture. "Microclimates often provide very narrow growing zones," she explains. "Even though plants can be quite adaptable to extreme conditions, some that do well in heat cannot take the below-zero conditions, and others that are hardy in cold temperatures may not be able to take the heat. Native plants tend to fare the best."

She suggests that high-altitude gardeners learn what's worked for other gardeners in the area. "Know the growing needs of plants before you buy them, then give them what they need in the way of soil, water, and exposure." She adds, "Don't take gardening too seriously. Make sure you are having fun. If all else fails, you can grow plants in pots. Take it from me, I've been there!"

MacLeod has learned firsthand that a region's elevation and climate determine what kinds of plants, trees, and shrubs will grow best there. Factors like temperature, humidity, precipitation, sunshine, and wind present opportunities for gardening fun and frustration. Successful Colorado gardeners can follow nature's lead and use our vibrant climate to their advantage. This chapter explains the growing challenges related to hardiness, elevation, and weather and provides tips for making the most of them.

Colorado's Hardiness Zone 5

Hardiness is an important indicator for plant survival and is dependent on geography. The U.S. Department of Agriculture (USDA) Plant Hardiness Zone map provides essential information for gardeners in the United States, Canada, and Mexico. You can access this map on the Internet at www.usna.usda.gov/Hardzone/.

The map is based on the average annual minimum temperature for eleven zones. Zone 1 (Fairbanks, Alaska) has an average minimum temperature of minus 50 degrees Fahrenheit. On the other end of the scale is Zone 11 (Honolulu, Hawaii), with an average annual minimum temperature of 40 degrees. The map is further divided into *a* and *b* regions. These represent 5-degree differences within each 10-degree zone.

For practical purposes, Colorado is considered Zone 5: an average minimum temperature of minus 20 degrees to minus 10 degrees. However, some parts of our state have areas that qualify as Zone 3, 4, 6, or even 7. The extremes rep-

Hardiness Zone by Zip Code

The National Arbor Day Foundation has a handy hardiness zone tool on its Web site (www.arborday .org). Simply type in your zip code to find the hardiness zone number for your specific area.

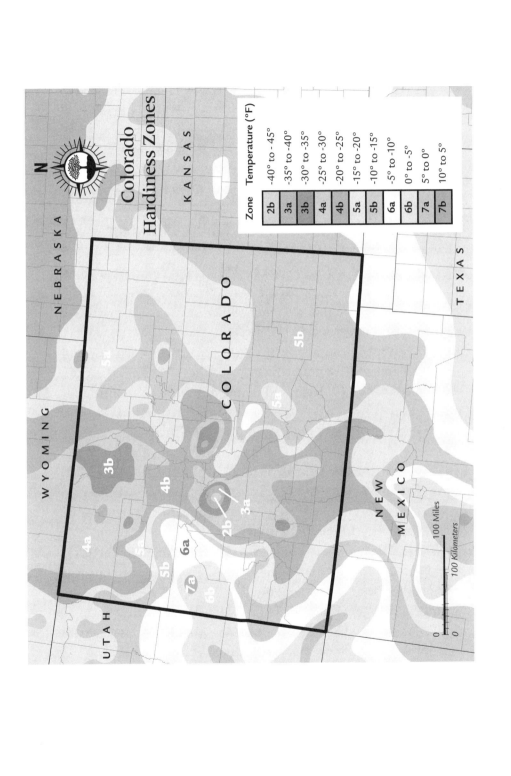

Colorado
Hardiness Zones

N

Zone	Temperature (°F)
2b	-40° to -45°
3a	-35° to -40°
3b	-30° to -35°
4a	-25° to -30°
4b	-20° to -25°
5a	-15° to -20°
5b	-10° to -15°
6a	-5° to -10°
6b	0° to -5°
7a	5° to 0°
7b	10° to 5°

WYOMING

NEBRASKA

UTAH

COLORADO

KANSAS

NEW MEXICO

TEXAS

100 Miles

100 Kilometers

0

0

resent small island zones that may be warmer or cooler than the area surrounding them because of differences in elevation.

If a range of hardiness zones is given for a plant, it means the plant is known to be hardy in each of those zones. For instance, if a perennial is recommended for growing in Zones 3–7, it can be planted in Zones 3, 4, 5, 6, and 7. When selecting plants by zone, take into account the fact that some plants may be perennial in Zone 8 but can be grown as a short-lived annual in our Zone 5.

Making the Most of Your Microclimates

The saying "cheaters never win" didn't come from a gardener. Shrewd gardeners know clever ways to cheat their hardiness zone. These determined gardeners know it's possible to grow a Zone 6b plant in a Zone 5a climate.

If you take a close look at a map of hardiness zones, you'll see the island zones within larger zones. These islands represent a difference of 5 or 10 degrees in temperature from the surrounding area.

On a smaller scale, our yards also have small islands of climactic conditions called microclimates. Understanding how to use the microclimates in your yard can make a difference in what, how, and when you plant.

I once talked with an experienced gardener who grew bushels of perfect tomatoes in the same spot in her garden, year after year. She said she always planted her seedlings on March 17, two full months before her area's last frost date. I tried to uncover her planting secrets, but the only clues she gave were to say she planted near a fence and used bricks to keep the plants warm.

My guess is that spot in her garden is an ideal microclimate for tomatoes. The fence and bricks must get full sun during the day and hold the heat to keep the plants warm at night. The fence probably acts as a windbreak and protects the seedlings from frost.

Most yards have a microclimate that provides superior

growing conditions to other parts of the yard. Temperature, quality of sunlight, soil conditions, drainage, and shelter from wind and extreme weather all contribute to creating a microclimate.

In my backyard there's a long, narrow strip of grass that stays cool during the hottest summer days. The grass in that part of the yard is always lush and green and doesn't use as much water as other parts of the yard. During the summer the house provides this area with shade while the rest of the lawn is exposed to sun all day, every day. I guess the rest of my lawn would look better if I only had a taller house.

Here are some ways to find the microclimates in your yard. Use your observation skills and take detailed notes to refer to later.

1. Complete an inventory of the planting spaces in your yard.

2. Observe areas where plants do especially well or especially poorly.

3. Note the types of plants that do well and that do poorly.

4. Determine the amount of sunshine each area receives from early spring to late summer.

5. Consider soil conditions (or take soil samples for testing).

6. Measure the amount of soil moisture by how easy it is to penetrate the soil with a screwdriver. If it penetrates easily, the ground is sufficiently moist. If it penetration is difficult, the soil is too dry.

7. Estimate the average amount of precipitation or irrigation each area receives.

8. Use a thermometer to measure the temperature in different areas of the yard (close to the foundation of the house, under a shady tree, next to a sunny fence, etc.).

Once you have your microclimate data, you can learn to be a cheater. During your observations you may have found "hot spots" in your yard. These could be areas close to the foundation of the house, higher on a slope, with a south-facing exposure, or near a heat-absorbing fence. The temperatures in these microclimates could be as much as 8 to 10 degrees warmer than other parts of the yard. Armed with this data you can experiment with plants that may be too tender for other parts of your yard. Planting close to a water feature, like a pond, provides added humidity.

Planting in the Hellstrip

One microclimate where plants like it hot is the planting area between the sidewalk and curb. It's such a devil of a place to landscape it's called a hellstrip. Weather extremes, water runoff, car exhaust, and foot and paw traffic make for difficult growing conditions.

The typical street strip features a patch of grass, a tree or two, and pop-up sprinklers that make for inefficient watering. Gardeners can make the most of this microclimate by creating a striking landscape that gives new meaning to the term curb appeal. Replacing the turf in the hellstrip with water-wise plants is also a big step toward water conservation.

Before tearing up the turf, gardeners should check to see if they need any municipal approvals. For instance, Denver residents living on designated historic parkways need approval from the Denver Parks and Recreation Department before starting any landscaping projects.

For the hellstrip microclimate, select plants with the same or similar needs for soil, moisture, and light conditions. Choose low-growing, drought-tolerant perennials with different bloom times, colors, and textures. Add stepping-stones or a path to reduce wear and tear. Native plants that thrive in a tough-love environment are perfect for the hellstrip.

Native plants for sun to part shade:
- Prairie zinnia (*Zinnia grandiflora*)
- Pussytoes (*Anetennaria rosea*)
- Poppy mallow (*Callirhoe involucrata*)

- Blanketflower (*Gaillardia aristata*)
- Blue mist penstemon (*Penstemon virens*)

Plants for a textural theme garden (sun to part shade):
- Snow-in-summer (*Cerastium tomentosum*)
- Lamb's ears (*Stachys byzantina*)
- Curlicue sage (*Artemisia versicolor* 'Seafoam')
- Blue fescue grass (*Festuca glauca* 'Boulder Blue')
- Sea urchin blue fescue (*Festuca glauca* 'Sea Urchin')

Ground covers for full sun:
- Creeping phlox (*Phlox subulata* 'Blue')
- Creeping basket-of-gold (*Alyssum montanum* 'Mountain Gold')
- Pink chintz thyme (*Thymus praecox* 'Pink Chintz')
- Creeping sedum (*Sedum spurium* 'Bronze Carpet')
- Starburst ice plant (*Delosperma floribundum* 'Starburst')
- Turkish veronica (*Veronica liwanensis*)
- Blue woolly speedwell (*Veronica pectinata*)

Ground covers for semishade to shade:
- Periwinkle (*Vinca minor*)
- Variegated big-leaf periwinkle (*Vinca major* 'Variegata')
- Bugleweed (*Ajuga reptans*)
- Variegated bishop's weed (*Aegopodium podagraria* 'Variegatum')
- White Nancy false nettle (*Lamium maculatum* 'White Nancy')

Elevation Affects Plant Performance

A summer drive across Colorado will give you a good idea of the diversity of the state's topography and weather. If you drive west on Interstate 70 from Kansas to Utah, you'll drive across warm dry plains, through foothills, over the chilly mountains of the Continental Divide, and down into the hot western valleys and plateaus. As you travel you'll also see each of Colorado's five plant life zones.

The life zones are based on elevation and are a guide to the plants that grow best in each zone. As you drive west, you'll climb in elevation from the Plains zone, 3,500 to 5,500 feet, to the Alpine zone, above 11,500 feet.

Pay attention to the changes in vegetation as you leave the plains grasslands heading for the hills. What you'll learn from

Colorado's Five Life Zones

Mother Nature has experience putting the right plant in the right place, and proof lies in the five Colorado life zones, or bioregions. These zones are used as a way to classify Colorado's plant life and can help gardeners grow plants where they naturally do best.

- The Plains life zone is prairie grassland, and it makes up almost half of the state. This life zone is found at elevations under 6,000 feet above sea level. Plant life here consists of grasses and shrubs that are adapted to higher temperatures and little precipitation.

- The Foothills life zone is considered a semidesert region and is located between 6,000 and 8,000 feet. It consists of ponderosa pine forests and woodlands.

- The Montane life zone is a denser forest, populated with Douglas fir trees, at an elevation from 8,000 to 10,000 feet.

- The Subalpine Forest, from 10,000 to 11,500 feet, serves as a transition zone that's called the tree line. Trees won't grow beyond this zone.

- The Alpine zone begins at 11,500 feet and is a treeless, tundra environment. This area receives the most precipitation and is markedly cooler than the other life zones.

your attention to vegetation is that in each life zone the plants have happily adapted to their environment. You'll see yucca, sage, pinyon pine, gambel oak, ponderosa pine, and a variety of wild perennial plants and flowers. When you reach timberline you'll have to leave the confines of the car to see the small alpine plants growing there. These little gems survive the strong winds that buffet their exposed home by hunkering close to the ground.

How to Use Elevation to Your Advantage

Perhaps you've heard the saying, "Bloom where you're planted." That's a good way to think about the plants, trees, and shrubs that grow best at certain elevations. As Coloradans we're fortunate because we can grow a wide variety of ornamental plants and shrubs. But plant performance depends on the differences in elevation and the resulting cooler or warmer climate. Higher elevations are naturally colder and have shorter growing seasons.

Many home owners living at lower elevations want to re-create the dazzling fall beauty of aspen trees in their own backyards. But aspens grow best in the Montane and Subalpine Forest zones. Gardeners often wonder why our state flower, the columbine, doesn't do well in plains gardens. That's because columbines grow best in the Alpine, Subalpine, and Montane life zones.

When you're making your planting selections, choose plants that will thrive in your area's natural conditions. The best way to do this is to observe the plants that grow naturally in the area and then copy Mother Nature.

There are many good resources to help make planting decisions. *Best Perennials for the Rocky Mountains and High Plains* is based on research conducted at CSU's W.D. Holley Plant Environmental Research Center in Fort Collins. Plants grown and evaluated there are the ones that flourish in Rocky Mountain and high plains landscapes.

Gardening in the Mountains

Gardening above 7,500 feet presents specific challenges. In addition to Colorado's low humidity and temperature fluctuations, mountain gardeners have to cope with poor soil conditions, shorter growing seasons, hungry wildlife, and wind. Here is a list of high-elevation plants, used with permission of Colorado State University Cooperative Extension, and recommended by Irene Shonle, Gilpin County director, and Laurel Potts, Eagle County horticulture agent. "There are just two things gardeners need to help them be successful in gardening in the mountains," says Shonle. "They need to exploit their microclimates and choose their plants wisely."

Herbaceous plants

†Prickly dianthus (*Acantholimon* spp.)

*Pearly everlasting (*Anaphalis margaritacea*)

*Pussytoes (*Antennaria* spp.)

Pigsqueak (*Bergenia* spp.)

Clustered bellflower (*Campanula glomerata*)

*Harebells (*Campanula rotundifolia*)

Dianthus 'First Love' and *Dianthus deltoides*

Dragon's head (*Dracocephalum nutans*)

Globe thistle (*Echinops* spp.)

*Showy daisy (*Erigeron speciosus*)

*Sulphur flower (*Eriogonum umbellatum*)

Sea holly (*Eryngium alpinum*)

*Wallflower (*Erysimum capitatum*)

Blanketflower (*Gaillardia* spp.)

Hardy geraniums (*Geranium* spp.)

*Prairie smoke (*Geum* [*Erythrocoma*] *triflorum*)

†Creeping baby's breath (*Gypsophila repens*)

Coralbells (*Heuchera* spp.)

†Candytuft (*Iberis* spp.)

*Native iris (*Iris missouriensis*)

Deadnettle (*Lamium maculatum*)

*Blue flax (*Linum lewisii*)

Maltese cross (*Lychnis chalcedonica*)

*Bee balm (*Monarda fistulosa*)

Catmint (*Nepeta* spp.)

*White-tufted evening primrose (*Oenothera caespitosa*)

*Scarlet bugler penstemon (*Penstemon barbatus*)

*Whipple's penstemon (*Penstemon whippleanus*)

Iceland poppy (*Papaver nudicale*)

Oriental poppy (*Papaver orientale*)

American poppy (*Papaver triniifolium*)

†Himalayan border jewel (*Polygonum affine* or *Persicaria affinis*)

Salvias (*Salvia* spp.)

Sedums (*Sedum* spp.)

*Golden banner (*Thermopsis divaricarpa*)

†Thyme (*Thymus* spp.)

†Veronica (*Veronica* spp.)

*Showy goldeneye (*Viguiera* [*Heliomeris*] *multiflora*)

Grasses

*Indian rice grass (*Achnatherum* [*Oryzopsis*] *hymenoides*)

*Tufted hair grass (*Deschampsia caespitosa*)

Blue avena grass (*Helictotrichon sempervirens*)

*June grass (*Koeleria macrantha*)

† = Ground cover

* = Native plant

Colorado's Wild Weather

Colorado gardeners should be prepared for everything when it comes to weather. We have four distinct seasons, but that doesn't mean they are predictable. Snow can fall on the mountains in June, hail can hit the Front Range in September, and early spring freezes can nip peach blossoms in the bud. Lack of precipitation in August singes turfgrass, but an early October blizzard breaks the limbs of trees still in full leaf.

The Western Slope has weather patterns so different from the Front Range it deserves a separate forecast by TV meteorologists. The temperature averages aren't that much different from the averages along the Front Range, but the weather is more consistent on the Western Slope. When it starts to get warm in the Grand Valley in spring, it usually stays that way.

The area around Grand Junction provides ideal conditions for growing plums, pears, peaches, cherries, and grapes. In the past few years, this part of the state has become known as Colorado's wine country.

On the other side of the divide, fluctuating temperatures create a freeze-thaw cycle that presents different growing conditions for Front Range gardeners. Denver can have a temperate 60-degree day in January followed by a snowstorm the very next day. Late spring frosts occur at the most inopportune times—when leaf buds have started to open or when fruit trees have blossomed, killing all chances for juicy peaches later in the season.

If you're a Front Range gardener, you'll need a little more planning, preparation, and patience than our gardening friends on the Western Slope. For instance, if you want to grow apples, pears, plums, cherries, and grapes on the Front Range, you can select hardy cultivars that do well with temperatures similar to those on the other side of the divide but that have a shorter growing season. CSU Cooperative Extension can provide recommendations for these hardy cultivars.

The National Oceanic and Atmospheric Administration's National Weather Service is a good resource for finding temperature forecasts for your zip code at www.weather.gov.

In addition to temperature, other weather factors include annual precipitation, frost-free days, snow cover, and severe weather.

Annual Precipitation

Colorado's precipitation is decidedly unpredictable. Many times residents in the mountains are still making snow angels in March while folks in lower elevations continue to wait for significant amounts of precipitation. "We really need the moisture" has become a cliché to gardeners from Fort Collins to Pueblo. Each year seems drier than the year before.

When storms start in the Pacific Ocean, they move eastward and lose moisture as they cross the mountains. The Front Range may or may not receive precipitation from these storms. Storms that move in from the north usually don't carry enough moisture to help with winter precipitation.

Our dry winters and low humidity can be particularly hard on perennial plants, trees, and shrubs. Dry winter soils can heave and crack, making roots vulnerable. Windy weather compounds the problem by desiccating roots. The damage won't show until spring when tree branches are dead and perennial plants are stunted or don't return at all.

The best protection is to select cold- and drought-hardy perennial plants, trees, and shrubs. You can also plan ahead for a lack of precipitation and little or no snow cover by adding extra mulch at the end of the season. Place mulch at least 4 inches thick to help retain moisture, to prevent soil cracking, and to protect roots from temperature fluctuations.

Check soil moisture throughout the winter months from October to February. Keep an eye on the thermometer and provide supplemental water when the air and soil temperatures reach 40 degrees, especially when there's no snow cover.

Watering during winter helps keep the roots of trees and woody shrubs from becoming dehydrated.

Trees need to be watered slowly to about 12 inches deep. Water early in the day to prevent the water from freezing on the ground. You can use a deep-root fork or needle, sprinkler, or soaker hose. Be sure to place the deep-root fork about 8 inches into the soil and move the water around the tree's dripline.

Lawns with south and west exposures will also benefit from winter watering. Shovel snow from sidewalks onto flower beds and around shrubs.

Chapter 3, "Water," provides more information about Colorado's challenging water situation.

Frost-Free Days Determine Growing Season

Depending where you live, you may have a growing season of 157 days along the Front Range, 190 days in the Grand Valley, about 140 days in the northeastern area of the state, and 90 days in the mountains. The growing season is determined by the number of days when the weather is frost free (above 32 degrees) and warm enough to support planting and growing. For many types of plants and vegetables, the growing season isn't long enough, so seeds are started indoors to give the plants a head start.

Spring is an especially fickle time of the year, and Colorado weather can play cruel tricks on gardeners. Despite the well-known unpredictability of spring weather along the Front Range, many garden centers stock pallets of colorful annuals in late April, relying on a gardener's eagerness to get planting the moment the weather turns warm. After a pleasant afternoon of planting petunias, that same night a killing frost is likely to destroy the day's efforts. Then back to the garden center we go.

Even when the thermometer reads 70 degrees, it's best to resist the siren call of early planting until after the last frost date. The last frost date is the final day in spring when the area might have a killing frost.

Here's one thing to remember about frost dates: Don't trust 'em.

The dates are only averages, based on years of weather data. May 2 is the last frost date for the Denver area, if you want a 50 percent confidence level of avoiding a killing frost, according to Colorado State University's Cooperative Extension. The longer you wait to plant, the higher the confidence level. May 18 has a 90 percent confidence level of avoiding frost, but keep in mind the weather-weary Denver gardeners of 1951. That's when their last frost date was June 2.

Colorado Springs, at an elevation of 6,035, has an average growing season of May 15 to October 10. But the earliest fall frost was September 3, 1962.

The last frost date for areas in the central Rocky Mountains, like Carbondale, can range from June 5 to 10. Areas in southwestern Colorado, like Durango, can have June frosts, too. In these areas gardeners delay planting outside or depend on a variety of plant protectors to keep plants warm during chilly times.

You can adjust the dates of the first and last killing frost for your area using elevation information. Use the frost dates for Denver and count forward or backward one day for each 100-foot change in elevation above or below 5,280 feet. This gives you the average frost date for your location. But remember, microclimates in your area can affect the amount of frost damage. A south-facing area of the yard may be able to withstand frost better than a low spot on the north side of the house.

Severe Weather Warning

Colorado weather can certainly be wild at times. Flash floods, lightning, thunderstorms, and tornadoes are just a few of the severe weather hazards Coloradans face. Mountain areas might be hit with blizzards and freezing temperatures while the plains remain dry. Spring storms can cause havoc on the eastern plains while weather on the Western Slope is mild. The state's main highways, Interstates 70 and 25, might be forced to close due to ice, snow, or wind—sometimes all three. Severe storm warnings and storm watches are frequently issued throughout the state during the spring.

But a discussion of Colorado's wild weather wouldn't be complete without mentioning hail. If you live on the eastern plains, whenever you hear the word *thunderstorm*, think *hail*. March usually signals the start of hail season, with June and July having the highest number of storms. Gardeners and their gardens are especially vulnerable during this time. At the first sign of lightning or thunder, gardeners should put down their shovels and go inside. Colorado is third in the nation for fatal lightning strikes.

The eastern half of the state is especially prone to severe hailstorms. The combination of where the plains sit in relation to the Rocky Mountains and clashing wind currents from the east are the ingredients for a perfect thunderstorm. The most damaging hail fell on July 11, 1990, in Denver. That storm caused $600 million in property damage. Limon, in the northeastern part of the state, has an average of seven days with hail each year. On the Western Slope, Grand Junction averages only one storm with hail each year.

Hail can turn a lush garden into shreds in only a matter of minutes. I remember one midsummer morning standing in my vegetable garden admiring my tomato plants. They were tall and loaded with blossoms. That afternoon those same plants were pummeled to the ground by a fast-moving thunderstorm that dropped enough hail to cover the ground. Other parts of the city weren't touched by the storm.

Even though my veggie garden was left in tatters, the rest of the landscape shrugged off the storm. The ornamental grasses were bent but not broken. Perennials, like agastache and penstemon, were missing only a few flowers, and the evergreens were just slightly bruised.

There was no hope for my tomato, pepper, or cucumber plants. Once the blossoms were crushed and the leaves shredded, there wasn't much left of those plants, although the shreds made good mulch. On the other hand, the basil plants were large enough to have intact leaves near the bottom. Petunias were cut back and other annuals pruned. If it were earlier in the season, I would have headed back to the garden center for a few replacement plants.

Hail is inevitable for gardeners living east of the mountains. Gardens that are already growing healthy plants will bounce back sooner than less vigorous plants. Here are seven steps you can take to protect your landscape:

- Select hardy varieties of plants, especially native plants. They're well adapted to Colorado's weather.

- Choose plants with narrow leaves that can withstand pelting rain and hail.

- Limit flowering plants that have large leaves. These are easily shredded in a hailstorm.

- Use natural features in the yard as protection for less-hardy plants. Sheltered areas near fences, close to the house, or under trees will protect smaller plants.

- Keep trees pruned to prevent damage to branches during severe weather.

- Build a solid cover to protect especially vulnerable areas.

- Keep protective sheets, blankets, or other covers handy to throw over containers or favorite garden crops.

As a last resort you can use the same method as gardeners in Cheyenne, Wyoming. Because the weather there is especially brutal—about nine hailstorms each year—hail-resistant greenhouses are the ultimate solution.

Water

Frederic Remington depicted many scenes of the American West in his paintings, but the one called *Fight for the Water Hole* is especially poignant. Created in 1903, the sparse prairie landscape shows five trail-worn cowboys, rifles drawn, protecting a small pool of water. This painting illustrates a grim reality about life on the old frontier. Water was worth fighting—and dying—for.

Fortunately those kinds of water wars are over. Now fights over water rights are waged in courtrooms. Our state's water laws are complex and the issue of water rights is confusing. For the typical gardener, terms like "doctrine of prior appropriation" and "senior and junior water rights" are best left to lawyers who specialize in dealing with water conflicts.

In other parts of the country, there's so much natural precipitation home owners don't need to irrigate their lawns. That's a luxury Colorado gardeners will never know. In years of higher-than-normal precipitation, our suburban landscapes can look luxurious because it takes just a little extra moisture to keep bluegrass green. The problems start when no extra moisture falls from the sky.

Gardeners may understand matters of water scarcity better than most. Only a gritty gardener knows what it's like to try to keep a landscape alive while following thrice-weekly watering restrictions in the middle of a scorching summer.

The state's annual precipitation is meager to begin with. We almost qualify as a desert. The annual average is just 17 inches, and that's the average for the entire state. Even though it's surrounded by mountains, the San Luis Valley in south-central

Colorado may receive only 7 inches of precipitation over an entire year.

During my master gardener training, I learned a lot about horticulture, but the most interesting topic dealt with Colorado's water issues. There were a lot of facts tossed around the classroom that day, but there's one fact that really stuck with me: There will *always* be a drought somewhere in Colorado.

Drought is cyclical, occurring about every twenty years, but 2002 went on record as one of the most severe droughts the state has experienced. Prior to that, the last dry times in Denver were from 1954 to 1957 and again from 1977 to 1981.

We're in Hot Water

While we have a somewhat wetter outlook than states in the Southwest, managing our water responsibly is still is a high priority. For the last several years, I've attended the Xeriscape Council of New Mexico's annual conference in Albuquerque. Each year I listen intently as water experts from across the country discuss solutions to our country's water issues. During a "Growth, Water & Sustainability" panel discussion in 2006, seven experts presented seven solutions for dealing with current and future water challenges. None could agree on the best approach.

I've seen movies depicting terrifying natural disasters, but no bit of fiction ran chills down my spine faster than listening to one of the conference presenters. Robert Glennon, professor of law and public policy at the University of Arizona and author of *Water Follies: Groundwater Pumping and the Fate of America's Fresh Waters*, said: "We can't make more water. All that is, is."

And when it's gone, it's gone.

Glennon said "Americans are spoiled" when it comes to water. He's right. When we turn on the tap, we expect clean water to come flowing out. But as more demands are placed on our shrinking water supplies, we can't afford to be spoiled any longer.

Production agriculture may account for the majority of water used in our state, but gardeners play an important role in managing water resources. If you garden in Colorado, you know that your landscape won't survive without supplemental water, but do you really want to use half your water outside during the summer?

Colorado gardeners can be better stewards of our water resources by reducing the amounts of water used in the landscape. Mandatory watering restrictions made a significant contribution to water conservation during our most recent drought. These restrictions, in addition to other conservation efforts, have led to a 20 percent reduction in Denver's water usage since 2002.

Home owners participating in a five-year Xeriscape study realized significant water savings. The YARDX (Yield and Reliability Demonstrated in Xeriscape) project, conducted between 1997 and 2002, was a collaboration of the U.S. Bureau of Reclamation and seven municipalities and water districts along the Front Range. The complete study results make for interesting reading at www.coloradowaterwise.org/yardx.htm.

Rainwater Harvesting Is a Muddy Issue

During times of watering restrictions, it may seem like a good idea to set a rain barrel under the downspout as a means of conservation. But don't do it without first checking with the Colorado Division of Water Resources and all local entities that might have a rule against it.

It boils down to this: The rainwater that falls on your property doesn't belong to you. In our state that water is considered part of the tributary to a natural stream and should be allowed to run off.

That said, it's difficult to get water experts to agree when discussing the nuances of Colorado's water laws.

"In most areas of Colorado, the only sure legal way to use rainwater is by positioning roof gutter downspouts to areas you wish to water," says the Colorado State University's Cooperative Extension. But in the words of a representative the Colorado Division of Water Resources, the agency responsible for protecting water rights, "It's in conflict with state water law to do that." We're not supposed to divert and hold rainwater.

Even though there are gray areas when discussing Colorado water law, there is one area of agreement: It's okay to divert your shower warm-up water into a bucket to water the rhubarb. However, using *gray water* in the landscape is a different story. Gray water is household wastewater from baths, showers, sinks, and washing machines. Permits to use large amounts of gray water are required from either the Colorado Department of Public Health and Environment (www.cdphe.state.co.us/cdphehom.asp) or your local health department.

Your city's local water department can answer questions about water rules in your area. For groundwater information and well permitting, contact the Colorado Division of Water Resources, Office of the State Engineer, http://water.state.co.us/groundwater/groundwater.asp.

For more information, contact CSU Cooperative Extension for fact sheet 6.702, *Graywater Reuse and Rainwater Harvesting.*

Water-Wise Gardening

After the drought we experienced in the late 1970s, members of Denver Water began thinking about the future. In 1981 they started the Xeriscape landscaping movement. The term *Xeriscape* comes from the Greek word *xeros* for "dry," and the goal was to get Coloradans thinking of ways to match our landscapes to our climate. Instead of trying to re-create the lush look found in landscapes along the East Coast, we needed to return to our native high plains roots.

Water-wise gardening has finally caught on. Now home owners fill large auditoriums to hear lectures on how to create xeric landscapes, and home owner associations are revising their covenants to allow for less lawn. Nurseries and garden centers are stocking more native and drought-tolerant plants. Improved drip irrigation systems are flooding the market. Information is available for replacing bluegrass lawns with native grasses, and Xeriscape garden tours are being offered in towns all over the state.

All of these efforts are helping to change the idea that Xeriscape means Zeroscape. Xeriscape means we're being realistic about living in a semiarid climate: We don't get much precipitation and probably never will.

Case Study: My Drop in the Bucket

When I moved into my suburban Denver neighborhood, I liked the look of the front yard just fine. There was a nice ash tree in one corner and a nice maple in the other. The rest of the yard was wall-to-wall green, and I had a heck of a time keeping it that way. Summers kept getting drier. There were no spring rains; no summer monsoon.

The summer of 2000 was a turning point. Because I'm a hose dragger, it took a lot more effort to keep my grass growing. I also had a feeling the water situation was going to get worse.

After admiring photos of yards with reduced lawns and colorful plants, I decided to try my hand at xeriscaping. My plan was to have a small peanut-shaped lawn surrounded by flowering, drought-hardy plants. A smaller lawn meant less hose dragging, less mowing, less work.

The next spring I paid to attend a Xeriscape Planning and Design program offered by Denver Water. The program included an informational seminar and a two-hour consultation with a landscape designer. To prepare for the consultation, I measured the yard, sketched it on paper, and took photos from every angle. Based on my photos and ideas, the designer drew a plan and recommended plants that would do well in each area of the yard.

Before planting could begin, I needed approval from my

home owners' association. The gas and water company were notified so the utility lines could be marked. Then I started digging up the lawn. I dug and dug and answered questions from curious neighbors. One neighbor thought I was installing a sprinkler system and was shocked—shocked—when I told him my hard work was part of a plan to use less water and not more.

A used copy of *The Frugal Gardener* by Catriona Tudor Erler was my guide to creating a garden on the cheap. Garden club plant sales provided a resource for inexpensive, but water-wise plants. Yellow yarrow, purple coneflower, and bearded iris plants were one dollar each, daylilies 50 cents a piece, and small sprigs of Mexican feather grass were a quarter.

That first summer I still had to water to get the plants established. The next year mandatory water restrictions went into effect.

Now my landscape is colorful and maintenance is easier. The yard uses less water and takes much less time to mow. The flowers attract bees and butterflies all summer. Birds enjoy the dried seed heads in fall. When it snows, little white clumps form on the tall grass plumes making the yard look like a wonderland.

Xeriscaping—It's a Seven-Step Program

My Xeriscape case study illustrates the seven basic steps to creating a water-wise landscape:
1. Design for water conservation.
2. Improve the soil.
3. Limit irrigated turf areas.

4. Irrigate efficiently.

5. Select water-wise plants.

6. Mulch to retain moisture.

7. Maintain the landscape.

Let's examine these in detail.

Step One: Design for Water Conservation

All beautiful landscapes begin with a good plan. There are many options if you're sure you want to do something but are not sure what you want to do. You can hire a landscape architect or designer for a consultation or a landscape company to take on the entire project. If you want to do it yourself like I did, you can get ideas by touring Xeriscape demonstration gardens, reading Xeriscape books, or studying garden design magazines. Software programs are also available to let you create a plan in the comfort of your home.

During the planning and design step, keep asking yourself, "How will this design help me use less water in the landscape while meeting all my other landscape needs?"

When you begin planning, consider the existing hardscape, such as the slope of the yard, sidewalks, paths, driveway, established trees and shrubs, downspouts, fences, electrical outlets, views, and other site characteristics. Consider the features of the landscape you'll want to keep, eliminate, or disguise. One home owner in Denver realized the only way to accomplish her Xeriscape goal meant digging up the sidewalk that led to her front door.

Think about sun exposure during the growing season. Determine which areas are dry and sunny, dry and shady, shady and moist, etc. That will influence your selection of plants.

Decide how you'll want to use the area in the future. Do you sit on the front porch in the evening or do you just want a nice welcome home at the end of the day? Is it an active area for recreation? If so, what kind? Will it be used for entertaining, like a green living room? Will you need to add trees for privacy or limit them for volleyball games?

One additional consideration is the amount of time you want to devote to maintaining the landscape. Xeriscaped areas may require less work, but they're not maintenance free.

Once you've thought through your plan, put it on paper. Create a landscape base plan that is drawn to scale. Measure the landscape and property lines. Include all the major elements, including the outline of your house, patio, fence, and sidewalk.

Step Two: Improve the Soil

The basics of soil were covered in chapter 1, including how to use soil amendments to improve soil absorption and retention. No matter what you'll be planting, adding one or two inches of organic matter tilled deeply into the soil will help encourage roots and get plants established faster.

Not all soil amendments are equal. The landscape consultant who helped me with my Xeriscape plan warned me about the kinds of soil amendments *not* to use. If the material in the compost isn't clearly identified, she advised me not to buy it. "Don't use compost containing mountain peat, sphagnum peat, high salt content, or unanalyzed soil amendments," she said. Colorado mountain peat is a nonrenewable natural resource that when harvested leads to environmental problems in the high country.

Some plants don't need fancy soils. Many of our hardy native plants can make themselves right at home if you simply loosen the soil for planting. That's one reason my 'Pawnee Buttes' sand cherry shrubs are happy in my yard's sandy soil.

Step Three: Limit Irrigated Turf Areas

Limiting the amount of irrigated turf in the landscape makes sense when xeriscaping. After all, the lawn is the most water- (and labor-) intensive part of the yard. Limiting turf areas includes thinking about how your family uses the turf space and considering turf alternatives.

Used effectively, Kentucky bluegrass makes a nice addition

to a xeric landscape. A small lawn still adds a refreshing spot of green, but it uses less water and fertilizer. A larger lawn area might be needed because it fits your family's lifestyle.

How much of your turf area is *really* used? Just because you've always had large areas of lawn, it doesn't mean you use the entire space. Consider reducing the amount of turf and replacing it with water-wise ground covers and shrubs. Some areas might become more usable if covered with flagstone.

Which areas of the yard are difficult to water? South- and west-facing yards, sloped areas, shade, corners, and narrow strips of grass are prime spots for a turf overhaul.

Another alternative is to replace thirsty bluegrass with drought-tolerant native grasses like dwarf fescue, blue gramma grass, or buffalo grass. These options are discussed in detail in chapter 8, "Lawns." The important thing to remember about grass is that if you're serious about water conservation, limiting turf is the place to start.

Step Four: Irrigate Efficiently

Consider that 40 to 50 percent of landscape irrigation is wasted because of poor irrigation system design, maintenance, and management. Just think of all that wasted water. To use our precious resource most efficiently, select the best irrigation method for your landscape needs.

Irrigate turf areas separately from planting areas. Watering the turf separately is the most efficient use of irrigation water. Also, turf is best watered with low-pressure, low-angle sprinklers, whether on a sprinkler system or the end of a hose. Lawn sprinkler systems are further discussed in chapter 8.

Create irrigation zones based on the plants' water needs. Trees, shrubs, flowers, and ground covers have different water needs, but all benefit from low-volume drip irrigation, soaker hoses, microsprayers, or bubblers for irrigation. These systems are easier to install than an in-ground sprinkler system. Irrigation kits can be purchased with tubing, emitters, and instructions for setting up your system. Several sprinkler system companies are marketing new products to meet the demand for consumers interested in xeriscaping.

Drip irrigation is the slow application of water to the garden using emitters located along lengths of plastic water line. The advantage to this system is it puts water close to plant roots and is easily controlled through a hose attached to a water tap.

Soaker hoses have perforations (instead of emitters) along the hose's length for watering. Soaker hoses are less expensive and easier to set up than a drip system.

Subsurface irrigation systems use drip tubes that are installed below the soil to water plant roots and reduce water waste.

Choose watering times carefully. Deep, infrequent watering encourages stronger, deeper plant roots. Don't water during the hours of 10:00 A.M. and 6:00 P.M. Adjust the controller on the sprinkler system to meet the landscape's needs in spring, summer, and fall. Maintain the irrigation system on a regular basis. Conduct an irrigation audit each year to make sure the system you use is in tip-top shape.

Don't water on a fixed schedule. Let the plants "tell" you when they need water. You can judge the condition of plants based on wilting or yellowing leaves.

Step Five: Select Water-Wise Plants

So many plants, so little room. Every year new plants are being released into the green industry that are perfect for our climate. Plant hunters continue to bring back drought-hardy specimens to add to our xeric landscapes. Plants that thrive in countries with climates similar to ours—like Greece, Turkey, Italy, and South Africa—are perfect additions to our flower beds.

I was in a large audience the day Panayoti Kelaidis, director of outreach at the Denver Botanic Gardens and a modern-day plant explorer, asked, "What if we had a drought and the plants didn't notice?"

Xeriscape means selecting plants that do well in our climate, whether they receive supplemental water or not. There are several "no-water" gardens located throughout the state that prove some plants do very nicely with the water Mother Nature doles out. (See chapter 11 for a list of gardens.)

Basic Watering Guidelines

Established trees need about ten gallons of water per inch of trunk diameter applied once or twice a month. Shrubs need about five gallons of water twice a month for new shrubs, five gallons once a month for small established shrubs, or eighteen gallons once a month for large, established shrubs.

What plants to use? Native plants are good first choices for a water-wise garden. They're already well adapted to living in our area. The general characteristics of xeric plants include smaller fuzzy or finely divided leaves, which make them less susceptible to being scorched by the sun. Spring-flowering bulbs, like daffodils, tulips, and crocus, aren't native to our region, but they are naturally xeric. Here are some of my favorite colorful, water-wise plants that just happen to be native to the Rocky Mountains and the Southwest:

- Blanketflower (*Gaillardia aristata*)
- Coneflower (*Echinacea purpurea*)
- Harebell (*Campanula rotundifolia*)
- Hyssop (*Agastache* varieties)
- Penstemon (*Penstemon* varieties)
- Poppy mallow (*Callirhoe involucrate*)
- Prairie zinnia (*Zinnia grandiflora*)
- Primrose (*Oenothera* varieties)
- Rocky Mountain columbine (*Aquilegia caerulea*)

Additional plant lists are available throughout this book in related chapters. Chapter 6, "Perennials," also includes information on the Plant Select program, Colorado's premier program for introducing plants especially adaptable to the Rocky Mountain region.

Beyond selecting colorful, water-wise plants, you should also:

Develop hydro zones. Xeriscape gardeners know to group plants according to their water needs. There are low-water and no-water xeric plants of every shape, size, color, and texture. Group those that use more water together and plant them in naturally moister areas of the yard, such as a depression near a downspout. Group less-thirsty plants in areas that naturally

receive more sun and less water. This method of grouping plants together is called hydrozoning and is an effective way of saving water while meeting each plant's water needs.

Group plants by use. Another way to approach water zones in your yard is according to use. For example, if you like to sit on the back patio after work each day, plant the most colorful and highest-water-use plants where you can admire them. The next zone can be farther from the house and include moderate-water-use plants. The zone farthest from the house could include the most drought-tolerant plants that make up a no-water garden. No-water gardens are watered at the time of planting and receive no supplemental water afterward.

Step Six: Mulch to Retain Moisture

Organic mulch, as discussed in chapter 1, is useful in the garden to reduce the number of weeds, maintain soil temperature, keep the soil from crusting, and fill in bare spots. Mulch is especially important in xeric gardens for minimizing evaporation. Organic mulches (wood based) are used in flower beds and inorganic mulches (rock based) are generally used around trees and shrubs. Gravel-sized mulch is good for collecting fast-falling rain and letting it percolate down to plant roots, thus eliminating runoff.

Layer mulch about 3 or 4 inches deep and plan on adding mulch as needed. Mulch can be applied directly on the soil or on a permeable weed fabric. Don't use plastic sheeting because it discourages deep root growth. Refer to chapter 1 for a complete discussion of using mulch.

Step Seven: Maintain the Landscape

Wouldn't it be great if there really were such a thing as a maintenance-free landscape? All landscapes need some kind of maintenance, and that's true of Xeriscapes, too. However, the bulk of the maintenance is in the first few years. By the third year there's less upkeep because the plants have filled in and there are fewer weeds to worry about.

General maintenance tasks include pruning trees and shrubs, cutting back perennials, raking leaves, deadheading spent flowers, adding compost and mulch as needed, fertilizing when necessary, and watering. It's the same sort of upkeep as in other parts of the garden, except you'll be using a lot less water than you have before.

For more information on the Xeriscape movement in Colorado, visit the Xeriscape Colorado Web site (www.xeri scape.org). Another good resource, no matter where you live, is Denver Water's Web site (www.denverwater.org). Both sites provide landscape ideas, photos, and how-tos for getting started.

Green Things

Vegetable Gardening 1-2-3

Many Colorado newcomers want to know the answer to the same question: "What's the secret to gardening here?" These are seasoned gardeners who've never before had trouble growing anything—in Virginia, Michigan, Wisconsin, or California.

As you've seen in previous chapters, a combination of poor soil, little precipitation, low humidity, and crazy weather all seem to conspire against the Colorado gardener.

In this chapter you'll discover some ways to overcome the challenges of vegetable gardening in a semiarid climate. After all, Native Americans lived in the desert and grew many crops such as corn, beans, and squash. You'll learn that starting a vegetable garden is nearly as easy as 1-2-3—planning, preparing, and planting. Planning includes deciding what you'd like to grow, what type of gardening space to create, and how it will be irrigated. Preparing includes getting the soil ready and starting seeds indoors. Planting includes placing seeds and seedlings in the garden and then mulching when planting is done.

Because there are so many elements working against your gardening success, you'll also need a strong resolve. A short growing season, drying winds, daily temperature extremes, damaging hail, and drought can make Colorado gardening seem like real work. But it's worth it.

Having a vegetable garden connects me to the soil more deeply than flower gardening. Stepping out the back door to pick a pepper to add to Saturday's scrambled eggs or to clip some basil for pesto are two of my favorite moments in the garden. My vegetable beds are small, but in them I grow asparagus, baby greens, cucumbers, chile peppers, several varieties of tomatoes, basil, zucchini, garlic, chives, fennel, oregano, parsley, thyme, tarragon, and mint. I'd grow more if I had the space and energy for it.

Before I plant the first seed in the garden, I stop to ponder the wonder of it. Within each papery pod is everything needed to become a seedling. Just add water and the amazing transformation begins.

1—Planning

Planning begins with the end in mind. What is the purpose of your vegetable garden?

I know gardeners who depend on their gardens to supplement the grocery budget for their large families. At the end of the summer, these gardeners are busy canning hundreds of jars of veggies, making fruit jams, and blanching corn for freezing. One of my friends once ruined her stove top by canning so many jars of salsa and spaghetti sauce.

Other vegetable gardeners prefer to grow just enough veggies to enjoy through the season and to share with neighbors.

That may be where we got the saying, "If you don't have any zucchini, you don't have any friends."

The best advice I can give about vegetable gardening is to be realistic about the size of the garden and how much time you'll devote to it. Vegetable gardens can be a lot of work. You can always start out small and add to the garden each year.

Find Full Sun

All vegetable gardens need sun. Select an area of the yard that receives at least six hours of sun each day. If the location of your garden includes both sun and part shade, you can plant cool-season crops like lettuce, radishes, carrots, and cabbage in the shadier section. Use the sunniest area for warm-season crops like corn, beans, tomatoes, and peppers. Other viney veggies definitely need full sun.

Select the Right Varieties

Many kinds of vegetables can be grown in Colorado, even at high altitudes. When selecting vegetables varieties, know the average length of the area's growing season (see chapter 2). Also consider how long it takes for vegetables to be ready for harvest. Sometimes this means selecting seed varieties with the shortest amount of growing time.

Early spring is the time to plant cool-season vegetables. These hardy vegetables, like broccoli, cabbage, lettuce, peas, spinach, and radishes, prefer cool temperatures and are often planted several weeks before the last frost date. Cool season vegetables can withstand 40-degree nighttime temperatures.

Just as their name implies, warm-season vegetables need warmer temperatures to grow. They prefer temperatures above 60 degrees at night and include tender vegetables like beans, celery, corn, cucumbers, and summer squash. Tomatoes, eggplant, peppers, pumpkins, cantaloupe, and watermelon are considered *very* tender vegetables and are usually planted several weeks after the last frost date, when nighttime temperatures are above 55 degrees and daytime temperatures are above 60.

One vegetable that's especially easy to grow in our area is spinach. This leafy green is good to grow and good for you. It can be planted in a range of soils, and some varieties take only a month or so from garden to table. For a continuous crop, seed every ten days from spring through summer.

Joan Hinkemeyer of Denver is a garden writer and former owner of a garden design business. She's been gardening in Colorado for thirty-five years and understands the challenges of gardening here. "Because the weather tends to get warm in February, March, and April, we tend to hustle the plants to get them in the ground. But we can get snow and frost as late as Memorial Day," she says. "That leads to a short growing season. In the metro area we can get snow the first week of September."

The unpredictable moisture is also a problem. "We have microclimates in Colorado and have to cope with deluges that cause powdery mildew or plants to rot out, or we get steaming temperatures—or both," she explains. "Then there's the wind that sucks the moisture right out of the soil. And the clay soil is more suitable for making adobe bricks than growing plants."

Hinkemeyer offers the following suggestions for coping with our growing challenges:

- Amend (amend, amend) the soil with compost; make sure soil is well drained.
- Use raised beds and create your own ideal soil conditions.
- Talk to experienced local gardeners.
- Read gardening books related to the Rocky Mountains; other regional books don't apply.

Front Range Planting Dates

Joan Hinkemeyer of Denver offers these general guidelines for planting vegetables on the Front Range. These dates are approximate, she says, and may vary from year to year depending on the weather.

- April 15—lettuce, onions, peas, spinach, kale, Swiss chard
- May 1—carrots, radishes, beets, cabbage, kohlrabi
- May 10—beans, corn, cucumbers
- May 15—melons, squash, okra
- Memorial Day—tomatoes, peppers (harden transplants before setting in the ground)

- Buy plants at a reputable nursery that understands what grows well here.
- Know each plant's needs and plant in the proper microclimate.
- Grow vegetable plants where they will do best, even if it's in the flower garden or in a container in a shady spot.
- Plant zucchini and string beans so you know you'll have something.
- Grow cherry tomatoes for guaranteed success; plant a couple of larger tomato varieties, too.
- Use floating row covers to protect tomatoes from intense sun.
- Pay attention to the plants so you'll know whether they're healthy or not.

One last word of advice from the experienced gardener:

"Accept failure because you're dealing with living things. You have to plan for a certain amount of loss."

Design the Garden Space

Your garden space and the kinds of vegetables you want to grow dictate the garden layout. If you're ambitious and have a large plot of land, you'll have plenty of space for several planting beds. But don't worry if you have limited space. There's a garden layout to fit just about any kind of garden you'd like to plant. The most common vegetable growing spaces are the row-style garden, the close-row or block-style, raised bed, square-foot garden, potager garden, and container garden. Each has its advantages and disadvantages.

Layout	Advantages	Disadvantages
Row-style: The traditional garden where crops are planted in long, single rows.	• Unlimited space. • Can accommodate crops that need more room. • Can use a variety of methods and mechanical equipment to work the soil.	• Can be an inefficient use of garden space. • Soil can become compacted when walking along rows. • Weeding is a regular chore.
Close-row (block-style): Crops are planted in blocks of vegetables in rectangular beds.	• Increases planting space and crop yield compared to traditional row-style layout. • Narrow beds are easy to reach across. Weeding can be done without compacting soil.	• Needs a rich, well-drained soil. • Requires frequent fertilization. • Overcrowded vegetables may increase plant disease problems.
Raised beds: Beds are raised above soil level and are usually 3 or 4 feet wide and 6 feet long.	• Efficient use of garden space. • Deeper topsoil encourages healthier plants. • Walkways between beds make cultivation easier. • Reduces weed growth and helps regulate soil temperature.	• Need 8 to 12 inches of rich soil to build up bed. • Soil may need to be retained with lumber, rocks, or other material. • May dry out quickly and need frequent watering. • Requires frequent fertilization.

Layout	Advantages	Disadvantages
Square-foot gardening: The garden is a garden bed (4 feet square) divided into 1-foot planting squares.	• Good first garden for beginners. • Good for smaller spaces. • Reduces amount of thinning and weeding • Squares are designed for a certain number of plants. • Uses less water.	• Limits the kinds and numbers of crops. • May need more frequent watering. • Lumber used in grids can break down over time.
Potager: A French kitchen garden; usually laid out with a center and groups of crop beds forming a pattern.	• Decorative; combines functionality with form. • Curved rather than straight lines. • Flowers, herbs, and vegetables are planted together.	• May not have room to work with tools or wheelbarrow. • May take more work to keep garden aesthetically pleasing.
Containers: Using containers instead of planting in the ground.	• Ideal for gardening in small spaces. • Portable. • Reduces amount of work and maintenance. • Easy to protect in case of bad weather.	• Limit to the kinds of crops to plant. • May need frequent watering and fertilizing.

Plan the Irrigation System

The plants in the vegetable garden will need from 1 to 2 inches of water per week during the growing season. Planning the irrigation system depends on a number of factors. Consider the following questions to decide on the most efficient irrigation system for your garden:

- What kind of plants do you want to grow?
- What are their irrigation needs?
- What is the size of the garden?
- What shape is the garden?
- What is the soil's water-holding capacity?
- What is the source of the irrigation water? (City water, well, etc.)
- Where is the faucet in relation to the garden?

The answers to questions like these can help you choose the best method for delivering water to the garden. For example, if you plan on a large garden with a variety of crops, you might want to irrigate with rotary sprinklers. Rotary sprinklers can cover large areas with a lot of water, but they may not be good for crops that don't like to get their leaves wet, like tomatoes and peppers.

If your garden is smaller, low-pressure spray-head sprinklers might be a better choice and a more-efficient watering method.

Drip irrigation helps conserve water and is used to water crops planted in rows, blocks, raised beds, or containers; it can be placed on a timer to make watering even easier. A different version of the drip irrigation system uses soaker hoses for watering the garden.

Another irrigation method is the tried-and-true garden hose with a spray attachment. This old-fashioned system enables gardeners to closely monitor their water use. A watering can produces similar results for much smaller spaces.

Whichever system you choose, just be sure it will allow you

to water the garden deeply each time. Wait until the first few inches of soil are dry before watering again.

2—Preparing

Remember the nugget of information in chapter 1 that promised to make a difference in your gardening life? Well, here's where that nugget comes in handy. The majority of plant growing problems start with the soil. Vegetable gardens need well-drained, loamy soil.

Soil preparation is key. Adding organic matter to your vegetable bed will make your gardening life easier. Mixing compost into the garden each season improves the texture of the soil and helps vegetable roots grow deeper and become stronger. Add only

Tea for Two

It's easy to brew a special "tea" for fertilizing seedlings and transplants. This tea gives plants soluble nutrients for a powerful boost. Compost can be substituted for manure in the following recipe.

To make:
1. Fill a bucket or container about one-third full with well-aged manure.
2. Add water to fill the bucket.
3. Let steep until the water turns the color of dark tea (several days).
4. Strain the liquid through cheesecloth or burlap into a jug or other container; seal with a lid.
5. Use solid material in the garden or add it to the compost bin.

To use:
1. Dilute a cup of dark tea with water to create a weak tea mixture.
2. Water plants with water, then apply the manure tea.

1 inch of compost to the soil each season. Dig the amendment in deeply, at least two shovels deep.

Fertilizer is also needed to meet the garden's nutrient needs in the form of nitrogen, phosphorus, and some trace minerals. Colorado soil generally has enough potassium. You can choose from a variety of fertilizers. Manufactured (chemical) fertilizer choices include dry fertilizer granules and liquid fertilizers. There are also specialty fertilizers each formulated for a specific kind of plant. Some gardeners prefer to use slow-release fertilizers in the forms of tablets or stakes. Organic fertilizers include bonemeal or blood meal, well-aged manure, or cottonseed meal.

When planting, apply fertilizer several inches away from the plant and use with care. Too much fertilizer may result in beautiful, but fruitless, plants.

Start Seeds Indoors

Starting seeds indoors is the best way for Colorado gardeners to get a head start on planting. Many gardeners order seeds from catalogs during the dark and dreary days of January. The arrival of seed packets guarantees that spring is on its way.

Growing plants from seed has its advantages. Seed packets are less expensive than purchasing plants, you can try vegetable varieties that aren't available locally, and you can help heirloom plants from becoming extinct.

Seeds for tender annuals, like tomatoes, can be started any time from mid-February to mid-March for planting in the garden after the last frost date. To determine when to start your seeds, count backward from the estimated planting time, allowing six to eight weeks to sow and grow.

Many gardeners plan on planting earlier by using plant protectors purchased from catalogs or garden centers. These plastic protectors use water to warm the soil before planting and keep seedlings toasty during chilly spring days and nights. If you'll be using a plant protector, start your seeds a bit earlier.

There are three basic steps to starting seed indoors: seeding, growing on, and hardening off.

1. Select the flower or vegetable varieties you want to grow. Sow seeds ¼ inch deep in a seed-starter potting mix.

2. Spray with a water mist and cover with clear plastic.

3. Set in a warm, dark place until seeds germinate.

4. Keep seeds moist.

5. When seedlings emerge, remove plastic; move to a sunny spot.

6. Transplant to individual containers when seedlings have two pairs of leaves.

Judging by the garden supply catalogs, there are an endless number of products that can speed this process along. Special seed-starting kits, trays, germinating mixes, heating mats, and fluorescent lights are promoted to ensure seed-starting success. One gardener I know has rigged a special lighting system in his basement to provide seedlings with sixteen hours of light each day.

As for me, I have good luck starting my seeds in little peat pots covered with plastic wrap. When the seeds sprout, I remove the plastic, move the seedlings to a south-facing window, and watch their progress every day.

When the weather is warm enough for planting outdoors, I help the seedlings get accustomed to the garden by placing them outside in a sheltered place for several days, gradually exposing them to the sun.

3—Planting

Planting time brings out the kid in me because I just love to play in the dirt. It's easy to get carried away and plant too much, so I limit myself to those veggies I know I can grow and then I add a plant or two of something I haven't tried before.

Because most areas of Colorado have a short growing season, tomatoes and peppers are two plants that do better as transplants than sown as seed directly in the garden bed. Vegetables that grow quickly, like cucumbers and zucchini squash, do best when sown directly in the garden. Carrots, radishes, and other root crops also prefer to be planted outside.

Some people swear by moon or lunar gardening. The thinking behind planting by the four phases of the moon is that the moon's gravitational pull has an effect on the ebb and flow of moisture in the soil and plants.

The *Farmer's Almanac* is one source to use for timing tasks in the garden. It's believed the best time to sow seeds of plants that grow above ground is during the light of the moon from new moon to full moon. From full moon to dark of the moon is believed to be best for planting crops that grow below ground, like potatoes, beets, and carrots.

Seed packets provide spe-

A Simple Germination Test

If you have vegetable seeds left from last year, you can conduct a simple germination test to decide if they're still good for planting. Put ten seeds on a paper towel, cover with another paper towel, and moisten the towels with water. Place them in a plastic bag and keep moist and warm.

After seven to ten days, check to see how many seeds have sprouted and multiply the number by ten. If this percentage is above 75 percent, you can use the remaining seeds instead of buying new.

Seed Sowing Made Simple

The basics of planting seed are simple. Place seed in the ground, cover seed with soil, and keep soil moist until seed germinates. However, for as long as people have been planting seeds, they've been trying to make the process easier.

Indians rolled their seeds in clay balls to protect them from sun, wind, birds, and other animals. The seed balls weren't planted but broadcast on top of the ground. Rain would melt the clay and start germination.

Seed balls are still used today in natural farming around the world. Garden supply catalogs advertise this ancient seed-planting method as a new technique for planting wildflowers and hummingbird gardens. Ambitious home gardeners can even try their hand at making their own seed balls.

Other products are meant to make the sowing process easier. Gardeners can invest in fancy steel planting stakes to help keep rows straight, instead of two sticks and some twine. Seed spacers and handheld seed dispensers help distribute the seed more evenly and reduce the need for thinning.

Seed tape and seed carpet come preseeded and eliminate much of the work of sowing seeds. Just cut the tape to fit the area, place it on the ground, cover with soil, and water.

cific guidelines for planting, but the basics include planting in rows or hills or by broadcasting seed.

- With row planting, shallow furrows are made in straight lines and seed is sprinkled along the furrow.
- Hill planting groups four or five seeds in a raised area; the sprouted seeds are later thinned to several plants.
- Broadcasting entails sowing seeds in a solid band, rather than in a single row.

Add Mulch

The final step in planting is adding a layer of mulch to the garden. Mulch is important because it helps retain moisture and keeps the ground cool during the hottest part of day. Mulch also discourages weeds, making it easier to maintain the garden.

Place mulch around plants several inches deep. Dried chemical-free grass clippings make good mulch if placed a few thin layers at a time. Another good garden mulch is weed- and seed-free straw. Avoid using wood chips because they take quite a while to break down in the soil and may cause problems when cultivating in the future.

A True Tomato Tale

I can't imagine a vegetable garden without tomatoes. Nothing compares to the first bite of a homegrown tomato still warm from the sun. In fact some gardeners will do anything to ensure a tomato crop.

When my in-laws, Ed and Shirley Pendleton, decided to take a short getaway to New Mexico early one spring, my mother-in-law couldn't bear to leave her tomato seedlings behind. So she put the pots in a box and took them along for the ride. She planned on keeping them in a sunny window of the RV and tending them just as she would at home.

She didn't count on the RV having transmission trouble near Albuquerque. The motor home broke down on the outskirts of the city, and Shirley and Ed had to find a phone to call for help. The closest building was a casino located a half mile away. Without giving it a second thought, Shirley put her little dog under one arm, her tomato plants under the other, and she and Ed hiked along the highway to the casino.

Those were well-traveled seedlings by the end of the trip. They saw the inside of a casino, went for a ride in a tow truck, and spent the night in an Albuquerque motel.

I heard they all had a wonderful time.

Tomato Tidbits

Tomatoes are one of the most popular garden vegetables in states across the country, and Colorado is no different. Colorado gardeners can have success in the tomato patch with a little planning and patience. Amending the soil, selecting disease-resistant hybrid varieties, and growing healthy plants will produce a good yield—if the weather cooperates. Tomatoes don't like weather that's too hot or too cold.

The two types of tomato vines are determinate and indeterminate. Indeterminate vines grow and produce tomatoes throughout the season; determinate vines stop growing when flowers appear. Both types of vines do well in Colorado. Determinate vines provide a full crop all at once and are good for growing in containers. Indeterminate vines continue producing until the first hard frost.

Here are some tips for growing top tomatoes:

- In Colorado tomatoes are usually planted as seedlings. Buy small plants that haven't blossomed yet. Before planting, remove some of the lower leaves from the tomato plant. Plant the seedling in soil up to the remaining leaves. This encourages deep, healthy roots.

- Plant seedlings only when the night temperatures are above freezing and day temperatures are 60 degrees or above.

- Look for VFN-resistant hybrid varieties. VFN means the plant is resistant to verticillium wilt, fusarium wilt, and nematodes.

- Tomatoes need nitrogen for vegetative growth and color, phosphorus for energy, and potassium to regulate physiological processes. Test your soil to see what amendments are needed.

- A favorite tomato for short growing seasons is 'Early Girl'. Other popular tomato varieties include 'Brandywine', 'Celebrity', 'Big Boy', 'Fantastic', and 'Big Beef'.

- At higher altitudes, gardeners may need to create a warm microclimate in their garden to ensure adequate tomato-growing time or plant in a greenhouse.

- There's no need to use red plastic around tomato plants; Colorado's light intensity is enough.

Growing tomatoes in Colorado is not without challenges. Once again weather presents a major problem by means of wide temperature swings that stress plants. Warm daytime temperatures can be followed by cool nighttime temperatures. Mild nighttime temperatures may be followed by hot morning temperatures that cause blossoms to drop. Cool weather at blossom time can cause deformed tomatoes.

Let's look at four common tomato problems and their solutions:

Early blight—Give tomatoes plenty of space for air to circulate. Create a strong trellising system to keep tomatoes off the ground. Avoid splashing water on tomato plant leaves.

Blossom drop—Prevent blossom drop during cool weather by using a spray or hormone product that helps blossoms set. Use floating row covers to protect from intense sun early in the day. The problem usually resolves when the weather improves.

Blossom end rot—In Colorado the dry, leathery brown spots on the tomato are caused by fluctuations in soil moisture, not by a calcium deficiency as happens in other regions of the country. Maintain even soil moisture during dry weather.

Sunscald—Protect tomatoes from exposure to intense sunlight by maintaining a healthy leaf cover or provide another method (floating row covers) for shading the plant and fruit.

Another problem to watch for on your tomato plants are hornworms. An adult hornworm is intimidating to look at—4 inches long, fat, and green. Hornworms can strip a tomato plant of all its leaves in just a few days. Watch for damage and take action quickly with a biological control like *Bacillus thuringiensis* (Bt) or an insecticide, both available at garden centers. Handpicking adult hornworms can also keep them at bay. (We'll talk more about plant diseases and insects in chapter 10.)

Herbs in the Colorado Garden

Planting herbs adds a flavorful dimension to the vegetable garden. Herbs can be used for cooking, drying, and making wonderful gifts. Herbs are also a fragrant way to attract pollinators to the vegetable bed.

The easiest way to decide what herbs to plant are those you use in your favorite recipes. If you love pesto, add several basil plants to the garden. Tarragon is a beautiful plant that also makes a tasty herb vinegar for summer salads.

Herbs are usually planted in a separate area of the garden, but they don't have to be. They can be used as ground covers or as edging plants. Herbs won't need as much water as the vegetables, but they appreciate full sun and a well-drained soil.

Most kitchen herb gardens include dill, basil, thyme, tarragon, oregano, and sage. But the herb choice is limited only by the gardener's imagination. A scented herb garden could include mint, lemon balm, lemon thyme, and rosemary.

Themed herb gardens make for some of the most beautiful container gardens I've seen. Plants are grouped together for a cook's favorite meals. Italian cuisine calls for herbs like parsley, Greek oregano, basil, and chives. A salsa garden features cilantro, jalapeño peppers, tomatoes, and garlic.

Tarragon Vinegar Recipe

Tarragon is a culinary herb used in traditional French cooking. It has a sweet, licorice flavor that makes it perfect to use in salad dressings. The tarragon I grow is French tarragon, and it's planted as a perennial in the back of my vegetable garden.

- For tarragon vinegar, snip and wash bunches of the tarragon while it is tender and has good flavor.

- Fill a jar (any size) with the tarragon bunches.

- Bring a pan of vinegar (white wine, white, or cider) to steaming, but not to a full boil.

- Pour vinegar over the tarragon to fill the jar; cover with a tight-fitting lid.

- Steep the vinegar for at least one week.

The vinegar is ready when the color has deepened and it has a nice herby smell. Use it in any salad vinaigrette recipe or alone with a good olive oil. For a homemade gift, strain the leaves and rebottle the vinegar in a decorative container.

Extending the Veggie Season

For some gardeners, the growing season is never long enough. They've taken it as a personal challenge to find ways to extend the growing season. The two important factors for extending the season in Colorado are 1) using a method to capture the soil's daytime warmth for use at night and 2) protecting plants from cold, wind, and frost.

Cold frames, fabric row covers, individual plant covers, plastic covers on grow tunnels, space blankets, and outdoor lights are devices used by creative gardeners who meet the weather challenge head-on.

Case Study: Plant a Seed, Grow a Gardener

It's a shame more people don't have the chance to plant a seed and watch it grow. I wish everyone could taste a tomato picked from their homegrown vine. Rosalind Creasy, gardener extraordinaire and author of *The Edible Garden*, laments the fact that Americans are raising a whole generation of children who have never eaten something they've pulled from the ground.

Creasy is working to get children closer to their roots. She replaced her California front lawn with a magnificent garden teaming with more than one hundred different varieties of flowers, herbs, and vegetables. She encourages the kids in her neighborhood to stop and yank a carrot from the garden or watch her chickens scratch in their coop. Her edible garden provides a new way for kids to think about their vegetables.

This is only one example of how gardening with children is gaining ground in many communities. Groups of volunteers are now working with nonprofit organizations to turn unused playground space into school gardens. Since 1985 Denver Urban Gardens (DUG) has helped turn the soil of unused space into vibrant community gardens. With the support of Denver Public Schools, DUG continues to plant the seeds of environmental stewardship throughout the metro area.

Today's school gardens continue the long tradition started by clever schoolmarms in the 1890s. Those old-time country teachers used their gardens to help students study nature, learn good work habits, and develop social skills.

Over the past ten years, school gardens have reappeared. Now they're used to teach math, science, weather, and the language arts. Students learn about nutrition and healthy eating while working in the garden. There's also plenty of physical activity involved in planting, weeding, turning compost, and completing other garden chores.

continued

If you have children, I hope you'll get them involved in your gardening activities. There are so many lessons a garden can teach.

For young children digging holes is a lot of fun, but planting quick-sprouting radish seeds and tasting the results offer a priceless learning opportunity. Sunflower seeds and beans fit nicely in little hands. Older kids can create garden journals to document their efforts. The whole family can get involved in the Plant a Row for the Hungry program simply by planting one extra row of vegetables to donate to a local food bank.

Not only will gardening help kids learn where broccoli comes from, but it's a step toward encouraging a vital connection to their community and to our environment.

I'm usually so tired of gardening by the end of the summer that I'm happy when the temperature starts to drop. The only time I've extended my gardening season was to pick green tomatoes remaining on the vine, wrap them in newspaper, and let them ripen on their own.

Annuals

Annuals are the equivalent of rock stars in the garden. They live fast and die young. These flowers add instant, vibrant color to our gardens, but they grow, flower, set seed, and die all in the same season. Annuals are a practical addition to Colorado gardens. There are hundreds of varieties to choose from, they are easy to grow from seed or as transplants, and they flower quickly and have a long blooming season. Colorful bedding plants can transform a yard neighbors call "too green" into one that stops them in their tracks.

Annuals are so versatile they can be used in just about any setting, from small spaces to large expanses. They're planted in raised beds, rooftop gardens, containers of every shape and size, window boxes, hanging baskets, and tabletop color bowls. Who doesn't love the look of a few posies planted around the base of a tall shade tree?

One of the biggest advantages of planting annuals is they can make the garden look different each year or the same from year to year. Every May I fill large containers with red, white, and purple pansies. On the Fourth of July, I add a few star-spangled pinwheels to the containers and then sit back and enjoy my patriotic floral display.

This chapter will help you make the most of your annual display. In addition to learning how to use annuals in your landscape, you'll learn about biennials, another valuable addition to the landscape. Biennials are plants that have a two-year growth cycle. Both annuals and biennials add color, fragrance, and depth to the flower garden.

New Introductions Keep Gardens Growing

Each spring I walk into my neighborhood garden center and ask the question every adventurous gardener wants to know: "What's new?" I'm usually overwhelmed by the answer. Rows of annuals in dazzling colors leave me weak in the knees. It seems there are hundreds of new annuals introduced into the green industry every year. With so many catalogs and nurseries touting amazing new additions, a gardener has to wonder, is any plant really new?

Some new plants are hybrids of established lines that offer bolder colors, improved disease resistance, or greater hardiness. Other new plants might be a superior variety of a plant that's been available for years. Even old favorites like 'Majestic' pansies have undergone improvements. Many new plants are species never seen before. Intrepid plant hunters continue trekking to remote locales seeking plants to bring back for propagation.

Although the basics of plant breeding are fairly clear-cut, getting a successful result can take years of experimenting and testing. Most seed and plant companies won't introduce their new cultivars into the marketplace unless they perform well at multiple garden trial sites. The trialing process helps prevent a potential plant disaster for the grower who thinks the new perennial will thrive in Zone 4 when in reality it grows best in Zone 8.

Colorado is a popular place for plant trials. Welby Gardens, grower of Hardy Boy bedding plants, holds annual trials for a variety of seed and plant companies in its Denver fields. All-America Selections, the oldest international testing organization in North America, uses the trial process to name winners among its new seed varieties. At these field trials, plants are evaluated based on qualities like growing habit, time of bloom, disease resistance, and whether the color stays vibrant or fades in our intense, mile-high sunlight.

Colorado State University's annual flower trial garden, located in Fort Collins, is also used by many plant and seed companies to evaluate the performance of new annuals. For instance, Ball Horticultural, the well-known plant breeder, producer, and distributor, conducts plant trials in collaboration with CSU. Ball is famous for launching one of the most successful new plant introductions in 1995 with the 'Wave Purple' petunias. Now there's a Ride the Wave family petunia in just about every size, color, and flower form.

After testing is completed, CSU names the "Best Of" winners from each growing season. These include Best of Show, Best New Variety, and Best Of in more than thirty individual categories. Trials held in our state provide objective results for gardeners like me who have a hard time deciding which new annuals to try. Knowing a plant passed a rigorous Colorado growing test before you buy it means you can have more success in your own flower beds.

Annual Requirements

Most annuals prefer full sun, but some thrive in dappled or filtered sun and others do well in shade. In general, annuals like a well-drained, reasonably fertile soil.

Annuals can be purchased as seed available from garden centers or mail-order catalogs or passed from gardener to gardener in seed exchanges. Seeds can be started indoors four to six weeks before the last frost date or sown directly into the garden in spring as soon as the soil can be worked. Annuals are also grown in greenhouse nurseries and can be purchased as transplants.

There are three categories of annuals to choose from: Hardy annuals (pansy, strawflower, calendula, sweet alyssum) are

planted just as soon as the soil has thawed; semihardy annuals (geranium, dianthus, marigold, petunia) are planted after the last frost, but when nights are still cool; tender annuals (coleus, cosmos, zinnia, impatiens) are planted after the last frost when the soil has had a chance to warm.

I usually buy my annuals from garden club plant sales starting in early May. Because it's still too soon to plant, I keep the plants in the garage at night and move them into a sunny spot during the day. I know one gardener who uses a little red wagon to help with this daily chore.

Using Annuals in the Garden: Form Follows Function

"Form follows function" is a principle of architectural design that can be used in the landscape, too. Deciding how to use annuals in the landscape makes it easier to select the plants that best fit the function.

Here are some of the many ways annuals can serve a function in the garden:

- Fill areas of the garden while waiting for perennials to grow.
- Frame a special garden feature like a statue or a fountain.
- Cover an arbor, camouflage a problem area, or create privacy.
- Add a colorful accent as a background color or along edges of sidewalks.
- Use as a border to create separate "rooms" or areas of the yard.
- Attract bees, hummingbirds, and butterflies to the yard.
- Cover a large amount of ground quickly.
- Use as a cutting garden.
- Create a themed garden.

If you just want to plop a petunia in a planter, you won't need a grand plan. However, if you have a larger project in mind, it pays to plot it on paper. I agree with the experts when they advise to start small. There's a lot of work involved with planting and maintaining large garden beds.

Plant a Moon Garden

A moon garden is one clever example of a themed garden that provides enjoyment throughout the evening and into the night. There are few rules for planting a moon garden. Simply select flowers that are white or nearly white and those that remain open after sunset. Be sure the plants receive adequate sun during the day.

Examples of annuals suitable for a moon garden include dusty miller, flowering tobacco, four o'clocks, moonflower vine, and all-white petunias, salvia, and vinca.

A moon garden allows gardeners a relaxing opportunity to enjoy the garden after hours. Some gardeners get creative by planting in moon-shaped crescent beds or adding indirect lighting and light-reflecting statuary.

Sometimes Cheap Is Expensive

Six-packs of bedding plants used to be available only at garden centers, but now annuals can be purchased at grocery, hardware, and discount stores. These plants may be less expensive than those sold at a garden center, but they may not have had proper care. Buying early in the season improves your odds of getting discount plants before they are neglected.

Look for healthy plants that aren't too compact or too leggy. Check to see if the plant is root bound or has suffered from too much or too little water. Avoid plants with yellow or curled leaves, which may signal insect problems. If you're looking for instant color, buy plants in 4-inch pots or larger. Select plants that have buds but aren't yet in bloom.

Gardening magazines and books provide plenty of beautiful landscapes to get the creative juices flowing. Just keep your preferences and landscape in mind as you draw your plan. Do you prefer the look of a rambling cottage-style garden or symmetrical formal beds?

Next, consider how the annuals will look when planted together. Think about color, height and width at maturity, bloom times, and foliage color and texture, too. It's best to avoid planting too many colors and too many different varieties together, unless that's the look you're going for.

Pick Your Palette

Color plays an important part in the garden design. Color can make a hot spot in the yard seem cooler or a small yard seem larger. One or two colors of the same plant massed together make a classic statement. A palette of pastels conveys a softer image.

The one design principle that comes in handy when selecting colors for garden beds and containers is a color wheel. The color wheel is used by interior designers for creating harmonious color schemes, and it can be used for planting schemes, too. The wheel is based on color relationships according to the color spectrum. If you were introduced to ROY G. BIV in science class, you're familiar with the concept behind the color wheel.

Picture the colors of the rainbow in a circle starting with red, red orange, orange, yellow orange, yellow, yellow green, green, blue green, blue, blue violet, violet, red violet. Certain combinations of these colors harmonize with each other better than other combinations.

To use the wheel select any two colors opposite each other or select any three colors that form a triangle. Four colors can also be used by selecting two pairs opposite each other to form a rectangle.

Colorado Gardeners' Favorite Annuals

- Ageratum
- Angelonia
- Annual salvia
- Annual bachelor's buttons
- Calibrachoa
- California poppies
- Celosia
- Cleome
- Cosmos
- Dianthus
- Ganzia
- Geranium
- Hyacinth bean

- Impatiens
- Larkspur
- Lobelia
- Marigold
- Nicotiana
- Pansy
- Periwinkle
- Petunia
- Portulaca
- Snapdragons
- Sunflowers
- Verbena
- Viola
- Zinnia

Preparing the Bed and Planting

If you're starting a new garden bed for annuals, here are the basics steps for preparing and planting:

1. Select your spot and make a clear edge for the bed by digging an outline with a shovel.
2. Till the soil and break any clumps.
3. Add several inches of compost or other organic matter and fertilizer.
4. Water plants well before planting.
5. Plant on a cloudy or overcast day.
6. Remove plants gently from their pots.
7. Loosen roots that are tightly compacted.
8. Dig a hole and set the plant in at its soil level.
9. Give plants plenty of space to grow; avoid overcrowding.
10. Overlap flower varieties so they seem to flow.
11. Fill the hole with soil and tamp the ground around the roots.
12. Mulch the bed to hold in moisture.
13. Water in and keep moist until the plant is established.

Continuing Care

Most annuals don't need much fertilizer, and some do best where the soil is lean. Gardeners have their choice of using either chemical or organic fertilizers (or both) in their annual beds. Chemical fertilizers can give plants a quick boost when they need extra energy; organics make for good soil additives.

Water needs will vary depending on the plants and where they are placed in the garden. In general, provide about 1 inch of water a week especially when there are periods without significant precipitation.

Remove the spent blossoms to encourage continued flowering through the season.

Container Gardens

Container gardens aren't just for gardeners living in small spaces. Containers add an extra dimension to any patio, balcony, and garden. The sky's the limit when it comes to container combinations. Depending on the plant selection, containers can provide several seasons of beauty.

Kris Higgins, comanager of the annuals and production department at Tagawa Garden Center in Aurora, has twelve years' experience gardening in Colorado. She says that container gardeners have extra challenges here. "We see customers choosing the wrong plant for their environment," she explains. "Part of this problem is the plant tag may say 'full sun,' but in Colorado that may not be true. Our arid, high-elevation, sometimes high-wind environment works against a plant that may be full sun in a low elevation and higher humidity region. We also see that the plants are not being watered properly or fertilized properly."

The best way to overcome these challenges is to ask questions, says Higgins. "Ask the nursery where you shop for guidance on sun requirements." At Tagawa, like most independent garden centers, the plants are displayed in separate areas for full sun, part sun, and shade. Special signage details each plant's care.

"Use your fingers as a gauge for when to water. When the soil has dried to your second knuckle, water deeply," she says. "Because we water so often we leach out all the great nutrition in our pots, so it's important to fertilize regularly and to follow the directions on the fertilizer label." But more fertilizer isn't necessarily better. "It's also important for gardeners to change the container soil every year. Bugs and diseases will overwinter in the old soil, and there's also little nutritional value left." She recommends composting the old soil and putting it back into the garden.

Here are Higgins's plant recommendations for creative containers:

Tall and spiky plants like canna, gaura, angelonia, or hormium (New Zealand flax).

Trailing plants like bacopa, Wave petunia, vines, and sweet potato vine. Unusual plants include trailing coleus and Fanfare trailing impatiens.

Rounding/mounding plants like geranium, osteospurmum, and diascia.

How to Plant a Container

1. Water plants before planting.

2. Select the container of your choice. Make sure it is clean and provides for good drainage.

3. Add potting soil or a soilless mix; stir in polymer water crystals and a slow-release fertilizer.

4. Place plants starting with tall plants in the center, cascading plants along the edge, and round flowers elsewhere to fill the container.

5. Set the planted container on bricks or blocks to encourage drainage.

6. Water and fertilize regularly.

7. Pinch spent blooms and clip foliage as needed.

Designing a Container Planting

Sometimes a container will call out for a particular color and shape of planting. For other containers the color, size, and shape of plants and the foliage is open for your interpretation. Just be sure the container, plants, and space are well suited for each other. Hanging containers also qualify as container gardens.

Vary the shape of the flowers, as well as plant heights, to add interest to the container. For a professional look, use an odd number of plants, like threes and fives.

One trick I've read is to place plants in their own pots into the containers. That makes it easy to change plants when one gets too tall or stops blooming.

Foliage plays an important part in the container planting. You can mix flowers with plants of different foliage textures. The shape of the leaf is important, too. I've seen containers that use foliage contrasts: for instance, small and large, fuzzy with glossy, or colorful foliage that matches the color of flowers in the container.

Annual vegetables, like ornamental peppers, can be added to containers, as can herbs and ornamental grasses. I've even seen small container water gardens or single-specimen plantings. Some of my favorite containers are those with cacti and succulents. The possibilities are endless!

Biennials Add Garden Interest

Biennials are the perfect plant for gardeners who like to go to seed. Longer lasting than an annual and less predictable than a perennial, ornamental biennials are one of the best investments a gardener can make. These plants with a two-year growth cycle have been known to keep gardeners on their toes.

Flowers, weeds, herbs, and even vegetables can be biennial. Biennial seeds germinate in the spring and spend the summer in the form of a low-growing rosette of leaves. During that first year, the plants are busy establishing leaves and deep, thick roots to help them survive the winter. Flowers are produced the second year, after which the plant usually dies. But because many biennials are such prolific self-seeders, they seem to grow on forever.

Carrots, onions, and beets are biennials, but their roots are pulled and eaten long before they can flower. Other familiar biennials are cups-and-saucers (*Campanula medium*), sweet william (*Dianthus barbatus*), Queen Anne's lace (*Daucus carota*), and wallflower (*Cheiranthus allionii*). Pansies (*Viola*) are also biennials and will reseed themselves under the right conditions. Biennial herbs include clary sage, angelica, parsley, and caraway.

Johnny jump-ups probably got their name from their habit of jumping up in unexpected places in the garden. You never know where this biennial will turn up each year.

Many ornamental biennials have a tall, stately form that adds structure to the garden. Longtime favorites like foxglove (*Digitalis purpurea*), with its bell-shaped flowers, and the round blooms of hollyhock (*Alcea rosea*) lend an old-fashioned cottage-garden feel when planted along a wall or fence.

Because biennials have colorful and showy flowers, they're often used as a complement to annuals, bulbs, and perennials. They can add a vertical element to container plantings. The foliage of some biennial herbs, like curly parsley, makes an attractive border in the annual garden.

'Moon Carrot', a 2005 Plant Select recommendation, is a biennial that can be enjoyed for its silvery blue, lacy foliage the first year and a succession of pale pink flowers the next. Moon Carrot tends to self-seed and can live longer than two years if planted in a protected area.

It's best to sow biennials in spring to give leaves a head start on the heat of summer. Sowing seeds two years in a row is the best method for getting flowers to continue blooming year after year. For gardeners who don't want to wait to see their first flower, another option is to purchase a greenhouse grown plant that's already in its second season and ready to bloom. More seedlings will appear the following spring.

Frugal gardeners may be drawn to the *Lunaria annua*, the money plant. This tall biennial has large, purple flowers that dry into seed pods resembling silver dollars. Gardeners can get their money's worth by leaving a few seed pods on the plant for next year.

Just like annuals, biennial plants have certain sun, soil, and water requirements. Hollyhocks need to be planted where they can get six hours of sun each day. Foxgloves can take some shade. Most biennials like a colder climate, but some, like canterbury bells, have a difficult time surviving our winters, so they're grown as annuals.

Perennials

The older I get, the more I appreciate the nature of perennial plants. In late winter, just when I'm beginning to think that spring will never return, I catch a glimpse of something green amid the brown. When I pull back the layers of leaves and mulch, I see a black-eyed Susan waking up to another season.

Perennials are the backbone of the flower garden. Unlike annuals, these plants grow through several seasons and can live for many years. The list of perennials is nearly endless and includes plant categories from ground covers to climbing vines and everything in between. Perennials come in all shapes, sizes, and colors. These dependable performers can be started from seed, cuttings, or division. Perennials are usually easy-care, low-maintenance plants that, once established, require minimal amounts of supplemental water.

There are two main types of perennial plants: herbaceous perennials and woody perennials.

Herbaceous perennials are plants that don't form woody tissue and that die to the base each year. In spring new stems grow from the plant's crown. Herbaceous perennials include flowering plants, vines, ornamental grasses, and ground covers. Plants that grow from bulbs, corms, tubers, or other underground systems are also herbaceous perennials.

Woody perennials are plants that develop a woody base or root system, such as lavender and Russian sage. Roses, trees, and shrubs are also included in this category. (Trees and shrubs are discussed in chapter 7.)

This chapter offers advice from experienced Colorado gardeners to help you prepare, plant, and maintain a perennial garden. With careful planning you'll be able to create a season of color in your landscape that stretches from early spring to first frost.

How to Create a Perfect Perennial Garden

One accomplished perennial gardener in Fort Collins says she gives a perennial three chances to flourish in her garden. If the first site doesn't work, she tries two more places in her garden before she gives up on the plant. She understands that it takes the right site to make a plant feel at home. Finding the right site in your Colorado garden means considering what kinds of plants grow best at your elevation and what kind of microclimates you have in your yard (see chapter 2). These two factors will determine which perennials do well in your landscape.

That's one of the messages reinforced by Carole Kastler of Camelot Design in Littleton. A member of the Associated Landscape Contractors of Colorado, Kastler has been designing Colorado gardens for more than twenty years. She says there are four steps to creating a perfect perennial garden: decide where you want your flower bed, prepare the area, select perennials that do well in Colorado, and maintain the garden for constant color. Here are her top suggestions for each step:

Step 1—Decide on the size and shape of the flower bed. Make sure there is a context to the setting. The flower bed should have a relationship to the rest of the garden. Add structure and vertical interest to anchor the garden in all seasons with tall plants like ornamental grasses, shrub roses, or specialty evergreens. Consider a flower bed that continues into dappled shade and then full shade. A strong background is essential for a great flower bed: A wall, trellis, or bamboo fencing enhances the setting.

Step 2—Delineate the area to be amended. Start with a weed-free area and add five yards of compost per 1,000 square feet. Till the amendments into the existing soil to a depth of 10 inches. Rake the area and add water polymers if desired. Set up a drip irrigation system with micromist sprayers or individual one-gallon emitters (two emitters per one-gallon plant).

Step 3—Plant perennials that do well in Colorado. Select plants by sun requirements, color, bloom time, water needs, and height. Plant in groups of three or more in odd numbers. There are many plants that do well in shade. Tall shade plants include hosta, skullcap, ragwort, goatsbeard, mallow, and lily. Medium-height plants that do well in shade include coralbells, bleeding heart, columbine, Himalayan sage, lady's mantle, and monkshood. Short shade-loving plants include sweet woodruff, creeping veronica, moneywort, periwinkle, Jacob's ladder, Irish moss, pincushion flower, and pearlwort.

Step 4—Maintain the garden for constant color. Water deeply and less frequently. Avoid spraying late at night to prevent fungal problems. Cut off dead flowers at least once a month to encourage new blooms. Leave foliage around plants for winter protection. In early spring remove debris from around perennials and add an organic amendment.

Perennial Requirements

Be sure to plant your perennials where you'll be able to enjoy them the most. In addition to locating the garden in a favorite spot, there are other site considerations. The top four are hardiness, sun requirements, soil requirements, and water requirements. When selecting perennials for your garden, group plants with similar needs together.

Hardiness. For perennials to be successful here, they need to be hardy to Zone 5 for most areas of the state, hardy to Zone 4 for mountain areas, and hardy to Zone 6 in the state's warmer locations. Bulbs that need a winter freeze (like allium, crocus, daffodil, and hyacinths) do especially well in Colorado.

Sun requirements range from full sun to dark shade—and all of the variations in between. Besides understanding the sun requirements of perennials, you need to know whether plants will get morning sun and afternoon shade, all-day sun or direct afternoon sun, or shade all day.

- Full sun—Six to ten hours of sun each day.

- Filtered/partial sun (can also be called part shade)—Four to six hours of sun with morning or afternoon shade.

- Light shade—Sun is indirect; area is shaded by a tree or structure.

- Medium shade—Trees provide shade to plantings underneath.

- Dark shade—Dense shade; in Colorado there are few perennials that do well in dark shade.

Soil requirements. Preparing the soil is crucial because perennials are meant to stay in the same garden spot for several years. If you haven't conducted a soil test, before planting is a good time

High-Altitude Performers

Only the strongest perennials survive in Colorado's highest elevations. Here are some hardy recommendations for gardeners at 8,000 feet and higher:

8,000 feet: 'Snow Angel' coralbells, 'Starburst' ice plant, winecups, princesplume

9,000 feet: 'Blue Velvet' honeysuckle, 'Colorado Gold' hardy gazania, Corsican violet, 'Denver Gold' columbine

10,000 feet: 'First Love' dianthus, Turkish veronica, golden banner, showy goldeneye, blue mist penstemon

to test for fertility, salt content, and soil texture and then amend the soil as deeply as possible with organic matter (see chapter 1). Make sure the perennial bed is well drained.

Water requirements. Because water is such an important consideration for gardeners in Colorado, it's wise to select plants that can thrive in xeric to very xeric conditions. Plants that like dry conditions, bright light, and warm temperatures will do well in Colorado perennial gardens. Check plant labels or catalog descriptions for each perennial's water requirements. Group plants together based on their water needs.

Most newly planted perennials need to be watered every few days to allow time for the roots to become established. Exceptions to this guideline are "no-water" plants. These plants (such as *Glaucium corniculatum* and *Salvia cyanescens*) are watered when planted and then receive no supplemental water during the growing season.

Selecting Perennial Plants

How do you decide which perennials to use in your garden when there are so many wonderful plants available? First decide how you'll be using perennials in your landscape.

Perennial beds can be used as foreground or background border beds. Perennials can be planted in island beds or interplanted with shrubs, annuals, and bulbs. They can be used to create a backyard habitat for butterflies, bees, and hummingbirds. It's easy to get carried away, so just be sure you have the time and desire to keep up with maintaining the beds.

Landscape experts recommend placing similar plants together in groups of odd numbers. For instance, plant the same variety of plant in threes using a triangular pattern to create a pleasing design. One technique used in perennial beds at the Denver Botanic Gardens is to repeat groupings of the plant varieties throughout the garden to create an effect that ebbs and flows. You can also create mass plantings with flowers of a single color or combinations of complimentary colors. Refrain from planting with too many different colors and textures; less is definitely more in the perennial bed.

Once you have the garden bed in mind, consider the plant qualities that are important to you and your landscape, such as color, form, size at maturity, bloom time, foliage, and drought tolerance.

The Plant Select Program

"If plants can grow in Colorado, they can grow anywhere" should be the slogan for Plant Select, the cooperative program between the Denver Botanic Gardens, Colorado State University, and a network of landscape and nursery professionals. Plant Select began in 1996 with the goal of recommending plants that are especially suited to the difficult growing conditions of the Rocky Mountain region.

Savvy gardeners know to look for the distinctive Plant Select red-and-orange sunburst logo on plant markers when shopping for new plants. Many of the plants also display the Xeriscape logo, indicating a water-wise selection.

Plant Select is based on extensive testing at demonstration gardens located in nearly every corner of the state. Plants are provided free to selected public gardens in exchange for information about the performance of plants under different conditions. Herbaceous and woody plants also undergo testing at CSU to determine cold hardiness, insect and disease resistance, ornamental features, and other important qualities.

For example, one of the most popular Plant Select recommendations is the ground cover *Veronica liwanensis* (Turkish veronica). This ground cover was introduced in 1997 and has many of the qualities gardeners and landscapers look for in a perennial. It can be grown at elevations to 10,000 feet, is hardy from Zones 3 to 10, likes both full sun and part shade, isn't picky about soil, and is xeric once established.

Perennial Bloom Times

To ensure continuous bloom throughout the season, choose a mix of perennials that will flower at different times, from early spring through late fall. Here's a sampling of plants that give color to each season:

Spring:
- Basket-of-gold
- Blue flax
- Lamium
- Creeping phlox
- Soapwort
- Sweet woodruff
- Hardy cacti and succulents

Summer:
- Agastache
- Campanula
- Coreopsis
- Daylilies
- Whirling butterflies
- Russian sage
- Salvia
- Lavender
- Sedum varieties
- Shrub roses

Fall:
- Agastache
- Aster
- Hardy mums
- Sunflower
- Salvia
- Solidago
- Sedum
- Ornamental grasses
- Zauschneria

Colorful Natives for a Water-Wise Garden

- Golden columbine
- Chocolate flower
- Blanketflower
- Bee balm
- Blue flax
- Penstemon varieties
- Poppy mallow
- Prairie coneflower

- White-tufted evening primrose
- Prairie smoke
- Black-eyed Susan
- Prairie zinnia
- Desert four o'clock
- Harebell

A complete description of the Plant Select program, including plant photos and descriptions, is found at www.plantselect.org.

Native Perennials

Native plants can be defined as those plants that were here first. Native herbaceous perennials, like pussytoes, purple poppy mallow, and Rocky Mountain penstemon, are naturally adapted to the harsh growing conditions in Colorado. Natives also require less of us as gardeners. Because they are well suited to growing here, they don't need as much water or fertilizer as other plants in the garden. They also provide a food source for our other natives, like bees, birds, and other watchable wildlife. Select native perennials based on your garden's elevation and sun, soil, and water requirements. See the "Colorful Natives for a Water-Wise Garden" sidebar for suggestions.

Weeding Out the Rumors on Roses

Roses are deciduous woody perennials, and growing them in Colorado can be a thorny task. Rumors about their temperamental nature have given them an undeserved bad reputation. Gardeners who think they can't grow roses here have probably tried planting bare-root roses or rose varieties that aren't well suited to our climate. Mary Kirby, a consulting rosarian and master gardener in Jefferson County, is able to bury four of the most common rose rumors:

Roses are too difficult to grow here. Selecting the right variety for our climate makes growing easier. "There are roses recommended for our area that do very well," Kirby explains. Shrub roses are hardy and can grow at higher elevations. She admits that hybrid tea roses are fussier, but that can be solved by choosing a planting site that gets at least six hours of sun each day.

Hybrid teas are grafted and should be planted with the graft (the bump at the base of the plant) 1 or 2 inches beneath ground level. "Protect with extra mulch in winter to hold in moisture. Winter watering is also very important," she says.

Kirby grows many roses, but her favorites include 'St. Patrick' hybrid tea rose, 'John Davis' Canadian Explorer rose, Griffith Buck's roses, and the 'Dortmund' shrub rose. "That one is almost indestructible."

Roses need a lot of water. "Roses aren't xeric, but they don't like to be overwatered either." Roses like a well-drained soil and don't like standing water. They need only about 1 inch of water a week, she says. Use a drip irrigation system or water the ground and not the leaves to prevent disease.

Roses need special soil. Roses don't need special soil, just a well-prepared soil. "I fill a wheelbarrow two-thirds full with garden soil and add one-third organic compost. I mix it well with a shovel and use that as a planting backfill," Kirby explains. She waits to fertilize until the rose blooms and uses an organic fertilizer like Mile-Hi Rose Food sold by the Denver Rose Society and at area garden centers.

Roses are too much work. "Roses are as easy to care for as perennials, but I get more pleasure from roses," she says. Because of Colorado's dry climate, we don't have as many problems with rose diseases like black spot. Kirby deals with insect pests as they occur. She doesn't spray for aphids, but she will take strong action against pests like the rose midge, which prevents roses from blooming.

"One of the biggest challenges I have with roses is keeping the deer off of them. Deer love rosebuds. They also love the tender canes and leaves." While a fence or other physical barrier is the best way to protect roses from deer, Kirby tried a method recommended by CSU Cooperative Extension for blending eggs with water and spraying plants every two or three weeks. "I was moderately successful with this last summer," she says.

For those intimidated by roses' reputation, Kirby suggests talking with other rose gardeners. "Learning from people who know how to grow roses saves frustration." She recommends contacting local rose societies, visiting the American Rose Society Web site (www.ars.org), and reading books like *Growing Roses in Colorado* compiled by the Denver Rose Society.

Planting Perennials

Allow adequate space so each plant has room to grow and room for you to cultivate between them. Plants are usually placed in the soil so that the root-ball is even with the existing ground. A fertilizer is usually added during initial soil preparation. A liquid or controlled-release fertilizer is also added in spring. Some gardeners rely solely on compost as a nutrient-rich topdressing instead. If you're planting a bed full of native perennials, they do best in *unamended* soil. Mulch conserves moisture and prevents weeds.

When is the best time to plant perennials? Many gardeners plant in a frenzy in spring, exercising that pent-up energy from winter. But fall is a prime time for planting perennials. "From my experience, fall is better for planting than spring," says Lauren Springer Ogden, a seasoned Colorado gardener, author, and nationally known garden designer. "It's a wonderful time of year for planting." Fall planting can begin the second half of August and continue until late September. Cooler nights are the signal for plants to redirect energy from supporting top growth to building strong root systems.

There are other advantages to planting in the fall besides giving perennials time to get established. Most perennials can be snatched up at bargain prices, and once planted they'll need less water and care. Crisp fall mornings also make the time spent outside more pleasant for gardeners. "The main issue with planting in the fall is there aren't as many plants available as in spring," Ogden says. Of those perennials remaining in nurseries and garden centers, however, 90 percent can be planted in fall.

One of Ogden's first gardening experiments, about twenty years ago, was planting a fall perennial bed in the hellstrip at her home in Windsor. She planted the bed with extremely drought-tolerant plants on the last day of August, watered them, and then didn't water again that fall. "When they came up in spring, they were ready to rock.

"Perennials that do well are the plants that grow in spring and are done blooming in July," Ogden explains. She warns against planting fall-blooming, heat-loving flowers such as zauschnerias, salvias, and agastaches. "They don't do well with fall planting because they'll be trying to bloom and won't set down roots."

Warm-season ornamental grasses aren't good selections, either. Large grasses, like miscanthus and panicums, stop growing in the fall and will die during the winter. But cool-season grasses, like calamagrostis and festucas, are fine for autumn planting.

Whether planting in established beds or starting new perennial beds, soil preparation is the same in fall as in spring, Ogden says. She recommends watering the plants when planted and then twice a week for several weeks.

Sowing perennial seeds in fall is difficult, so Ogden recommends collecting seeds at the end of the season and keeping them in a cool place like the garage or fridge. Sow the seeds in pots in late December and put the pot outside around New Year's Day, she advises. Thin the plants when they come up in April or May. In June repot into small, individual containers. Plants will be ready to place in perennial beds that fall.

Ogden is an experienced hand with this method. Each year she sows 200 species from seed to use in a variety of landscaping projects. Not every attempt is successful; about 160 to 170 plants come up, she says. "I grow from seed when I want to experiment, when I can't get a certain plant locally, or when it's too expensive to buy plants in large quantities." She says there's no point in growing perennials from seed if the plants are available in a nursery. For gardeners wanting to save money by starting their perennials from scratch, Ogden recommends any of the one hundred garden-worthy penstemons. "There are about seventy to eighty varieties that you can't find locally."

Maintaining the Perennial Bed

Most flowering perennials have few maintenance requirements, and those tasks vary from season to season. For example:

Spring—Remove extra layers of mulch; clip any foliage and stems left from the previous season. Cut back ornamental grasses to a few inches above the ground. Prune rose canes. Water deeply as needed. Thin crowded plants and transplant seedlings that have self-sown; divide plants like daylilies when new growth emerges. Weed as needed. Add new mulch.

Summer—Water deeply as needed. Deadhead to remove spent flowers and to prolong bloom time. Dig and divide iris rhizomes. Stake tall plants. Weed as needed.

Fall—Water as needed. Add extra mulch in November. Clip stems or leave as mulch for winter. Plant spring blooming bulbs, if desired.

Winter—Provide supplemental water if there's no significant amount of precipitation.

How to Attract Bees to Your Garden

If you want a beautiful, productive garden, you need to attract bees. Honeybees are the best of the insect pollinators, but our bee populations are in serious trouble. Loss and fragmentation of habitat and use of chemicals, like insecticides and herbicides, are key reasons why bees are threatened. In addition, honeybees are falling victim to two kinds of parasitic mites.

There are simple steps you can take to increase the bee population in your garden. One step is to leave a number of dead branches for giant carpenter bees, leaf-cutter bees, and mason bees to nest in. Another is to stop using chemicals in the garden. If you must use insecticides, follow label guidelines, spray at night when pollinators aren't active, or use chemicals less toxic to bees.

The whole family can get involved in creating a bee habitat by planning the three elements that attract bees to the garden—food, water, and nesting sites.

Bees prefer flowers that are rich in nectar and pollen.

Bee Friendly

Here is a list of perennial flowers for bee-guiling:

- Black-eyed Susan
- Blanketflower
- Prairie coneflower
- Western wallflower
- Asters
- Dianthus
- Lavender
- Sage
- Bee balm
- Mint
- Cosmos

Select native varieties that are well adapted to the area's climate and soil. Choose a variety of colors, shapes, and scents, especially blue and violet flowers. Read plant labels carefully and avoid modern hybrids, including those with double and triple flowers.

Be sure to provide a source of clean water, such as a bird-bath, water garden, or shallow dish. Nesting sites may be the most important part of a bee garden for native bees. Nests can be as simple as leaving a small patch of bare ground in or near the garden for ground-nesting bees. Mason bees can be encouraged to stay in the garden if there's a supply of mud they can use as a building material for their nests.

With the right combination of colorful perennials, you can create a garden that is a continuous beehive of activity.

Trees and Shrubs

Pity the poor trees in our semiarid state. Intense, high-altitude sunlight, extreme fluctuations in temperature, lean soil, and drying winds create a most inhospitable environment. Because trees have such a difficult time growing in Colorado, every day should be Arbor Day here.

The advantages of planting trees are obvious—they protect us from the summer sun, shield us from the wind, and help save energy. They reduce air pollution and increase property values. We know that trees are a vital component of our environment, but most of us take them for granted.

If perennials are the backbone of the garden, trees and shrubs provide the structure. This chapter will explain ways to overcome the challenges of planting and maintaining trees in our harsh climate. You'll learn how to select and maintain trees—and shrubs—that match your landscape needs. To make this chapter easier to use, it's divided into two sections: The first part is all about trees and the second is about shrubs.

Trees

The average life expectancy of a landscape tree is less than ten years because of where and how it's planted. That's a sad statistic for a plant that does so much for us. If you're going to invest the time and money to add a tree to your landscape, be sure to expend the extra effort in planning, planting, and maintaining it to ensure the tree has a long, healthy life. One key is matching the right tree to the right place.

Planning

There are basically two kinds of trees: deciduous trees and conifers. Deciduous trees are trees that shed their leaves each year, like an oak or ash tree; conifers are evergreen trees like pine, fir, spruce, and other cone-bearing trees.

Before adding a tree to your landscape, consider its purpose, the qualities you're looking for, and where you want to plant it. There really is a tree for every landscape.

Purpose in the landscape. Trees serve many purposes in the landscape, and knowing that purpose makes all the other tree decisions easier. Ask yourself, "What do I want from my trees?" Possible answers include:

- Provide shade.
- Serve as a windbreak.
- Use for noise abatement.
- Function as a privacy screen.
- Add a focal point or accent.
- Provide food and shelter for wildlife.
- Add interest to landscape.
- Use for activities (like tree climbing, building a tree house, or hanging a hammock).
- Define property boundaries.
- All of the above.

Site location. A tree needs to be part of the overall design in your landscape. When evaluating the site, consider how the tree will balance the design, amount of sun the tree will receive, soil conditions, air circulation, irrigation, and drainage. All of these considerations are important, but the top concern is determining if there is enough space for the full-grown tree. The mature size of a tree depends on its form, height, and spread. Some trees can grow as wide as they are tall. Will your location support the space needs of a mature tree? The small spruce that looks adorable right next to the house when planted will eventually overtake the space and make it impossible to open the front door.

If you're planting a tree to create shade, determine what area needs to be shaded, at what time of day, and in which seasons. Select a site that's relative to the sun's angle and direction.

Keep in mind what will be beneath the tree and above it. Trees attract birds, which can cause a mess below the tree; then there's leaf drop in fall. Make sure trees won't grow into or above utility lines, either. Tree limbs can cause electrical outages if they crash onto utility lines during our typical late spring snowstorms.

If you're planting more than one tree, allow enough room so they won't crowd each other. Keep large shade trees about 40 feet apart, medium trees about 30 feet apart, and small trees about 25 feet apart.

Tree qualities. Each tree has characteristics related to its species. Which tree qualities are most important to you?

- Evergreen or deciduous
- Short or tall
- Upright, round, or spreading
- Interesting fruit, flowers, cones
- Leaf shape and color during the seasons
- Bark color and texture
- Fast or slow growing
- Longevity
- Pest and disease resistance/tolerance
- Maintenance requirements

There may be a trade-off when selecting trees based on these qualities. For example, if you want a tree that will immediately provide shade, you'll need a tree that grows quickly. But fast-growing trees are usually more brittle and can be prone to storm damage. They often don't live as long as slow growers, and they can be susceptible to insect and disease problems.

Some species of trees aren't recommended for sites along the Front Range because they won't perform well in that climate. Refrain from planting aspen, silver maple, birch, and elm. Look for alternatives that satisfy the desired tree qualities.

Large trees also take more time to become established in the landscape. In USDA Hardiness Zone 5, trees take about one growing season per inch of trunk diameter to become well rooted. This means that a larger, 3-inch-diameter tree will need three years for its root system to establish. A 1-inch-diameter tree would take only one year. The sooner a tree becomes established, the sooner it can start growing into a healthy tree.

Finalizing Your Tree Selection

As part of the planning process, you've considered a tree's mature size, shape, soil conditions, and potential pest problems. Now that you're ready to make a final selection, choose trees that are hardy for our climate and naturally tolerant of dry conditions. These are two keys to tree-growing success. See the "Xeric Trees" sidebar for one expert's recommendations.

Faced with rows of trees at the nursery or garden center, which particular specimen do you select? Many decisions go into selecting a tree, but the easiest decision is to *never* buy a tree with a codominant trunk. A codominant trunk means the tree has more than one trunk of the same size. Most storm damage to trees in Colorado is caused when one of the codominant trunks splits or breaks. I've seen trees sliced in half when one trunk is sheared off during a heavy snowfall.

Planting

Most people are surprised to learn that planting problems kill more trees than all insects and diseases combined. Usually trees are planted too deeply. Sometimes they receive too much water. Many times they're left to fend for themselves.

So let's get to the root of the matter about planting trees. Roots aren't just a tree's anchor to the ground; they're the tree's lifeline. Roots need room to spread out and they need oxygen to survive. Without adequate rooting space, a tree's growth will be limited. The root zone on a tree is like a wide, flat saucer. Roots are found in the top 12 to 18 inches of soil and spread out horizontally about 1½ to 2½ times the height of the tree.

As you plant a tree, follow these steps to reduce transplant shock and encourage root growth:

1. Dig a saucer-shaped planting hole that is at least three times the size of the root-ball. The hole should be shallow (no deeper than the root-ball) and wide. Remember that planting too deeply slows root growth.

2. Set the root-ball on undisturbed soil 1 to 2 inches above the soil grade.

3. Make sure the trunk flare is visible; cover the rounded area of the root-ball with backfill soil.

4. Water and mulch over the root-ball.

Maintaining the Tree

Because a tree is a major investment, care after planting is critical to its long-term survival. Trees growing in a dry climate and plagued with temperature extremes require even more care. Common problems include too little or too much water, sunscald, and cold-weather injury. Let's look at each.

Cultivating Fruit Trees in Colorado

The Grand Valley is known for its fruit production. Peaches, cherries, pears, and apples thrive in the more predictable climate found on the Western Slope. With a little extra planning and patience, backyard gardeners on the Front Range can also grow fruit trees. Here are some tips:

- Select a dwarf or semidwarf trees.
- Select trees that bloom after your area's last frost date.
- Cover trees when frost is anticipated.
- Plant in a sheltered area in the landscape; protect from wind.
- Select hardy cultivars that can survive cold winters to 20 below zero:
  - ✔ Johnathan, Gala, and Winesap apples
  - ✔ Bartlett and Bosc pears
  - ✔ Montmorency sour pie cherries
  - ✔ Imperatrice and Lombard plums
- Plant two different varieties to assure pollination, unless the trees are self-pollinating.

Watering and Overwatering

Trees suffer from drought injury when they can't take up as much water as is lost through transpiration, or the process by which water evaporates from leaves. After you plant a new tree, be sure to provide enough water to ensure adequate root-zone moisture for its first two years, especially during a prolonged dry spell—no matter what season. Check soil moisture levels with a water meter both at the root-ball and in backfill soil. Water trees slowly and deeply, to a depth of at least 12 inches. Saturate the soil around the tree's dripline (the outer edges of the tree's branches). For a newly planted tree, apply about two gallons of water per inch of trunk diameter twice a week; for established trees, use about ten gallons of water per inch of trunk diameter during each watering.

Avoid overwatering. Roots can't get enough oxygen in waterlogged soil.

Fertilizing

Newly planted trees won't need fertilizer until the second growing season. During the first-year establishment phase, it's more important to encourage root growth than stimulate leaf canopy growth. In fact, if fertilizer is added to backfill at planting time, roots can be damaged.

Established trees usually signal when they need to be fertilized, but a soil test is the best way to confirm it. Smaller leaves, lighter-colored leaves, and leaves falling early in the season are signs that the tree may need feeding. Fertilizers include those spread over the root zone and those applied below the surface of the soil. The soil test will show what nutrients are available or are needed, and this will help you select the correct fertilizer. Apply fertilizers when roots are growing, from spring to early summer.

Pruning

Properly pruned trees will be healthier and more resistant to insects and diseases. Here are some general pruning guidelines:

- Newly planted trees should be pruned only to remove broken branches or to keep a single trunk to the top of the tree.

- For established trees (three to ten years old), prune dead branches, crossing branches, and branches with weak crotches.

- For mature trees (fifteen years or older), conduct hazard pruning; prune for cleaning, thinning, raising, or reducing the crown.

- Never cut the top off a tree in an attempt to reduce the height of a tree.

A trained and experienced arborist is the best source of information for pruning trees. Two resources are the Internationalist Society of Arboriculture (www.isa-arbor.com) and the Tree Care Industry Association (www.natlarb.com).

Preventing Sunscald

Colorado's intense winter sun can scald the bark on young trees. One way to prevent sunscald is to plant thin-barked trees in protected areas that shield them from late southwestern afternoon sun.

You can also protect new trees against sunscald by applying tree wrap from November until April. A good way to remember when to use tree wrap is "Put it on at Thanksgiving, remove it around Easter." Another protective option is painting the trunks of young trees with a white, interior latex paint. Dilute the paint with water (1:2) and apply.

As always, be sure to provide adequate water to all trees during the fall and winter months.

Preventing Cold-Weather Injury

It seems that either an early fall or a late spring frost hits the eastern plains. Leaves turn black or brown where frost injury occurs. Selecting hardy trees and planting them in areas that are less susceptible to frost are two ways to prevent frost injury. Healthy trees are able to bounce back from frost damage better than trees that are stressed from disease or drought.

Another type of cold-weather injury is caused by heavy snowfall when trees are in leaf. There have been many spring days when I've found myself outside with a broom, gently brushing snow from tree limbs to keep branches from snapping off.

Trees also can suffer from diseases and insect injuries. You'll find information about these in chapter 10, "Coping with Pests and Plant Diseases."

Plant a Tree

Groups throughout the state continue the fine tradition of planting trees. The Colorado Tree Coalition (www.coloradotrees.org) has a shade-tree distribution program that provides trees to municipalities and community groups. Many communities have spring tree distributions for their residents. For example, Denver Digs Trees (www.theparkpeople.org) has worked since the early 1990s to distribute hundreds of trees each year at reduced prices. This adds to the thousands of public trees the group has added to the Denver landscape over the years.

Contact your local parks and recreation department or county extension office for information about tree-distribution programs in your area.

Shrubs

Shrubs are some of the most versatile plants in the garden. The lilac bushes that continue to bloom near abandoned prairie homesteads are a testament to their resiliency.

Shrubs are an essential design element in our gardens and can provide four seasons of interest in the landscape. They can be used as single specimens, in a mixed perennial border, and as a hedge or privacy screen. Low-growing evergreens are often used as ground cover. Shrubs can make an immediate impact in the garden, growing to maturity in three years.

Shrubs are woody plants that have multiple stems. Just like trees, there are deciduous and evergreen shrubs.

These Are Shrubs, Too

Some plants that you might not think of as shrubs are called sub-shrubs:

- Cotton lavender
- Honeysuckle
- Potentilla
- Thyme
- Lavender
- Cotoneaster
- Yucca
- Waxflower

Planning

The process for determining the purpose, location, and qualities of a shrub is similar to the process for trees. One of the major considerations for a shrub will be its height at maturity. Planning for height will narrow choices of shrubs for your landscape. There are tall shrubs (8 feet and taller), medium (5 to 8 feet), small (3 to 5 feet), and very small (under 3 feet).

In addition to height, consider:

- Water requirements
- Requirements for sun/shade
- Tolerance for alkaline soil

- Maintenance (Some require regular pruning.)
- Evergreen or deciduous
- Foliage and bloom color
- Shape and form
- Fragrance
- Fruit
- Attractive bark

Planting

Shrubs are installed in the spring as soon as the soil is dry enough for planting. Here are the basic steps for planting:

1. Water the shrub before planting.
2. Allow enough space for the shrub's mature height and width.
3. Dig a planting hole that's the same depth as the shrub's root-ball and about twice its width.
4. Loosen the soil and amend with compost.
5. Lift the shrub from its container and carefully loosen its roots.
6. Place the shrub so the top of the root-ball is even with the soil surface; spread the roots in the planting hole.
7. Fill the hole and firm the topsoil.
8. Make a saucer-shaped basin to retain moisture.
9. Mulch around the shrub, but keep mulch away from stems.

Maintaining

All new shrubs, even xeric ones, will need regular watering to keep the root-ball from drying out until the roots are established. Older shrubs will need about 1 to 2 inches of water each week, depending on the variety. Be sure to provide water in dry winters, especially when there is no snow cover. Newly planted shrubs

Xeric Shrubs

Scott Skogerboe, head propagator at Fort Collins Wholesale Nursery, recommends these xeric shrubs:

- Colorado manzanita (*Arctostaphylos x coloradoensis*): 1 to 3 feet
- New Mexican agave (*Agave neomexicana*): 1 to 2 feet
- Saskatoon serviceberry (*Amelanchier alnifolia*): 3 to 10 feet
- Leadplant (*Amorpha canescens*): 3 to 5 feet
- Silver fountain butterfly bush (*Buddleia alternifolia argentea*): 5 to 8 feet
- Bluestem joint fir (*Ephedra equisetina*): 3 to 5 feet
- 'Kintzley's Ghost' vine honeysuckle (*Lonicera prolifera* 'Kintzley's Ghost'): 6 to 12 feet
- Yellow-fruited chokecherry (*Prunus virginiana xanthocarpa*): 10 to 16 feet
- Wavyleaf oak (*Quercus undulata*): 5 to 18 feet
- 'Gwen's Buffalo' currant (*Ribes aureum* 'Gwen's Buffalo'): 6 to 8 feet
- 'Crandall' clove currant (*Ribes odoratum* 'Crandall'): 4 to 6 feet
- 'Autumn Amber' trilobed sumac (*Rhus trilobata* 'Autumn Amber'): 1 foot and lower

  Other water-wise shrubs include blue mist spirea, rabbit-brush, sumac, barberry, burning bush, lilac, and viburnum.

won't need fertilizing until the second growing season. Fertilize in spring with a slow-release fertilizer.

Some shrubs will need to be pruned annually or as needed to keep to a manageable size and to promote growth. Other shrubs do perfectly well without any pruning. When you prune is important. The worst times to prune most shrubs are when the shrub is in full leaf, when its leaves are falling, or when the weather is too cold.

Spring-flowering shrubs, like lilac and forsythia, bloom on the previous year's growth. Prune these shrubs in late spring as soon as the flowers fade. Summer-flowering shrubs, are pruned in early spring before they start growing.

Pruning can rejuvenate older, over-grown shrubs. Redtwig dogwood shrubs benefit from a spring pruning to remove broken or weak branches and to clean out crossing branches or those lying on the ground. When pruning, cut as close to the ground as possible and make the cut straight across.

When pruning older, heavy interior growth, you can prune up to 20 percent of the older branches. You can also reduce the height on deciduous shrubs by removing old canes at ground level or by shortening and making the pruning cuts at different levels along the stems.

Like trees, shrubs can be vulnerable to disease and insect problems. See chapter 10.

A Hardy Shrub Recommendation: Cheyenne Mock Orange

The mock orange has a long and interesting history. For many years this tall, fragrant woody plant grew next to the Clearwater River in Idaho. Native Americans used its straight stems for bows, arrows, tobacco pipes, cradles, and combs. In the early 1800s the shrub received its botanical name, *Philadelphus lewisii*, as one of the nearly 200 plant species first recorded on the Lewis and Clark expedition and named after its discoverer, Capt. Meriwether Lewis.

Often called Lewis's mock orange, *Philadelphus* refers to

Native Shrubs for High Elevations

- Curl-leaf mountain mahogany (*Cercocarpus ledifolius*)
- Mountain mahogony (*Cercocarpus montanus*)
- Fernbush (*Chamaebatiaria millefolium*)
- Rock spirea (*Holodiscus dumosus*)
- Creeping Oregon grape-holly (*Mahonia repens*)
- Western chokecherry (*Prunus virginiana*)
- Golden currant (*Ribes aureum*)
- Wax currant (*Ribes cereum*)
- Boulder raspberry (*Rubus deliciosus*)
- Silver buffalo berry (*Shepherdia argentea*)

Philadelphia, the City of Brotherly Love. There are sixty-five deciduous shrubs under the genus *Philadelphus* and many cultivars. The plants range in height from 3 to 10 feet tall. They vary in flower clusters and leaves. But only one variety is a Plant Select recommendation.

The Cheyenne mock orange, *Philadephus lewisii,* received its name because it was tested at the USDA Horticultural Field Station in Cheyenne, Wyoming. The station originally had two 400-foot rows of different mock orange species from around the world, but the cultivar originally from the northernmost part of Alberta, Canada, proved to be the most cold hardy.

Cheyenne mock orange is a good choice for Colorado landscapes. It is hardy in Zones 3 through 9 and can be grown up to 8,000 feet in elevation. It can be used alone in the landscape as a low-maintenance ornamental shrub, or it can be planted in a group and serve as a tall hedge. It blooms from late spring to early summer, and its fragrant flowers are reminiscent of orange blossoms. This shrub is xeric once established. It isn't picky about soil conditions or how cold it gets in winter.

Lawn

Most people forget that lawns are made up of many individual plants. We could do ourselves a favor if we started treating lawns more like the perennial ground cover it is instead of a piece of old green carpet.

Colorado gardeners have ideal conditions for growing turfgrass. Our cool nights and warm days are conducive to growing lush lawns. When managed properly a lawn is not only beautiful, but it helps keeps us cool in summer. Instead of reflecting heat, the lawn absorbs it. A healthy lawn is a work of art—with the emphasis on work.

Lawns are the most labor-intensive design element in the landscape. In our climate lawns need some kind of care during all four seasons. Fertilizing and irrigating start in spring; mowing in the summer; fertilizing in the fall; watering during dry winter months.

Less is more when it comes to turfgrass these days. Lawns, like gardeners' attitudes, are changing. Now the emphasis is on reducing turf areas or replacing thirstier turfgrass varieties with lower-maintenance species.

This chapter provides basic practices for managing turfgrass in your landscape. You'll learn about turfgrass alternatives, how to start a new lawn, mowing guidelines, and proven methods for effective irrigation in our dry climate.

Select a Turfgrass Species

Kentucky bluegrass is not native to our semiarid climate, but it performs well here. Bluegrass does have high water needs in the summer, but it's a tough grass that can go dormant and survive without water for long periods of time.

A variety of other turfgrass species also perform well here. But before you dig up your bluegrass and replace it with something else, consider all the factors. For example, how is the lawn used in your landscape? What size lawn do you need? How much maintenance are you willing to put into your lawn? What are the typical weather conditions in your area? What problems are there with soil or pests? What is the cost and availability of water for irrigation? All of these questions can help you clarify your turfgrass maintenance requirements.

Chapter 3, "Water," described seven steps for turning a landscape into a Xeriscape. The third step is *limiting irrigated turf areas*. This is accomplished by reducing the amount of irrigated turf, replacing Kentucky bluegrass lawns with an alternative turfgrass species, or both. Some of the grass alternatives, like buffalo grass, use less than half the water of a bluegrass lawn. However, buffalo grass has grayish green leaf blades. Gardeners who plant buffalo grass have chosen water conservation above having an emerald green lawn.

Turfgrasses are divided into cool-season and warm-season species. Cool-season grasses are green from March until November. Warm-season grasses are green from May until September. Turfgrass also has two growing habits: sod-forming grass that spreads by stolons or rhizomes and bunch grass that grows in clumps instead of forming a sod.

Naturally, you'll want to select turfgrass that is best suited to your site. The following table compares five different species.

Turfgrass species	Description	Supplemental water requirements
Kentucky bluegrass	Cool-season turfgrass. Grows by roots from single plants to form a dense sod.	About 2 to 3 inches per week
Blue gramma grass	Warm-season bunch grass.	About ½ to ¾ inch every two weeks
Buffalo grass	Warm-season, sod-forming grass.	About ½ to ¾ inch every two weeks
Tall fescue	Cool-season bunch grass.	About ¾ inch every week
Dwarf fescue	Cool season, sod-forming grass.	About 1 inch per week

Other turfgrass alternatives include perennial ryegrass, crested wheatgrass, and alkaligrass. Some creative gardeners have also planted thyme lawns. Bermuda grass is a warm-season grass that does best in warmer areas in the southeastern and western areas of the country. Zoysia grass is not recommended for use in Colorado because it isn't tolerant of our cold winter temperatures.

Grass-Growing Basics

Lawns can be grown from seed, sod, or plugs. Soil testing is always a good first step, whether you're starting a new lawn from scratch or working on a lawn that has always had problems. Soil test results may help narrow your turfgrass selections. For example, Kentucky bluegrass doesn't grow well on salty soil.

Starting from Seed

The ideal time for seeding cool-season grasses is in late summer or early September. The best time for mountain areas is in midsummer. Here are the basic steps for starting a lawn from seed:

- Conduct a soil test; add fertilizer or amendments as needed.
- Prepare the area by removing rocks and debris.
- Spread seed uniformly over the prepared site.
- Lightly rake seed into the seed bed.
- Irrigate to keep soil moist, especially after seed germination.
- Reduce the frequency of water as the seedlings form a root system.
- Irrigate deeper and less frequently to encourage a deep root system.

Starting with Sod

Spring and fall are the best times to plant sod.

- Conduct a soil test; add fertilizer or amendments as needed.
- Prepare the area by removing rocks and debris.
- Moisten the soil lightly before transplanting the sod.
- Water the sod frequently so that the underlying soil is always moist to encourage root growth.

Starting with Plugs

Some grasses, like buffalo grass, are easier to start from plugs instead of seed. Information about planting grasses using this method is found at the Web site www.highcountrygardens.com.

Dale Langford's Secrets to a Beautiful Lawn

Area lawn and garden expert Dale Langford has more than fifty years of experience gardening in Northglenn, Commerce City, and Aurora. Here are his top-ten secrets for growing a beautiful Colorado lawn:

Watering

1. Develop a program of watering deeply and seldom to help sod root deeper. This results in a stronger, healthier lawn that's able to cope with heat and drought.

2. Set timers to start sprinkler systems around 3:00 A.M. This allows you to water at a time with less wind and evaporation. As the sun comes up, the grass will dry and there will be less chance of developing fungus and other lawn diseases.

3. Apply wetting agents found in products like Revive to assist water to penetrate dry or heavy clay soils as well as just average soils. This product also has plenty of available iron to promote a deeper green color.

4. The easiest way to test moisture in soil is with a 6- to 8-inch screwdriver. In a lush, well-watered area, the tool will penetrate easily. In dark-colored grass or brown areas, it will go down a couple of inches and then feel like it has struck cement. In overwatered areas, the blade will simply sink to

Fertilizing

Bluegrass lawns have high nutrient needs in the form of either a natural organic or synthetic fertilizer. Other grasses, like tall fescue and buffalo grass, have lower fertilizer requirements.

Nitrogen is an essential nutrient. Lawns suffer when there is either too much or too little nitrogen in the soil. Low turf quality and an increased number of weeds are two problems associated with too little nitrogen. Excess nitrogen results in the need for

the handle. These tests can guide you to the proper timing for watering.

Mowing

5. Mow high (2½ inches) to encourage stronger plants that are better able to withstand summer's heat and drought.
6. Mowing higher also encourages more side growth to thicken the turf and keep weed seeds that blow in the yard from touching the soil and germinating.
7. Keep mower blades sharp to prevent browning from "whipped tops." Sharp cuts reduce lawn stress.

Fertilizing

8. Apply approximately four pounds of available nitrogen per 1,000 square feet of lawn throughout the growing season. Choose lawn foods that contain iron as well as nitrogen, phosphorus, and potash.
9. Liquid organic soil treatment products that incorporate effective horticultural wetting agents assist and supplement regular fertilizer, making nutrients more available to the plants.

General Care

10. A good aeration with 3-inch plugs removed (prewet the soil) in the spring or fall—or both—will open up the soil to improve air and water movement and stimulate side growth for thickening.

increased irrigation or a yellowing of the leaf blades called iron chlorosis.

Apply fertilizers to cool-season grasses in fall and late spring; avoid fertilizing during the summer. Fall is the most important fertilizer application for the lawn. Feeding at this time helps the grass bounce out of dormancy faster in spring because of early root growth.

Warm-season grasses are fertilized in early summer only.

There's no need for fall or early spring fertilizing because feedings during those times encourage weed growth.

Select a fertilizer that releases nitrogen slowly. Buy the brand of fertilizer specified for the spreader and follow the recommended settings. Because most Colorado soils have a pH range of over 7.0, your lawn may need a supplemental iron source, such as iron sulfate or iron chelate. These products are applied to turfgrass blades when the lawn starts to show symptoms of iron chlorosis (a patchy yellowing). If you properly apply a balanced fertilizer and leave lawn clippings after mowing, you probably won't need to add phosphorus.

Mowing

Height and frequency are the two important elements of mowing the lawn.

Resist the urge to mow your lawn below 2 inches in height. When lawns are mowed lower, roots can be severely damaged or killed. Grass that is kept about 2 to 3½ inches tall is healthier and thicker. It will also use less water because the soil is shaded and roots will be allowed to grow deeper.

Don't take too much off the top during any mowing. Remove only one-third of the grass blade each time. The one-third guideline helps prevent the lawn from being scalped and will maintain turf root growth. This may mean mowing more than once a week, but the lawn will be healthier for it.

A mulching lawn mower is a good choice for a healthier lawn, too. Mulched grass left on the lawn recycles nutrients to the turf. And there are fewer bags of grass clippings in the landfill. Leaving grass clippings has the added benefit of reducing the amount of fertilizing.

Compaction and Thatch Control

Some gardeners believe that leaving grass clippings on the lawn after mowing is the cause of thatch accumulation. This is not true.

Thatch is a layer of dead and living roots, stems, and grass blades that accumulate on the soil surface. This spongelike layer prevents water and fertilizer from reaching grass roots. Managing thatch means a healthier lawn.

Power raking is one way to remove thatch, but sometimes this can cause problems by damaging the turf layer. Core cultivation, also referred to as aerating, is an alternative. Core cultivation controls thatch and also relieves compacted soil—one of the factors that leads to thatch.

You can rent a machine or hire a lawn maintenance company to aerate your lawn in spring and fall. Plugs of grass are extracted at regular intervals over the lawn surface. Each deep hole provides a way for oxygen, water, and fertilizer (and sometimes grass seed) to reach the roots.

Irrigation

There are two parts to irrigating effectively: sprinkler system performance and water management practices. Unfortunately, most people believe that automatic sprinkler systems take care of themselves automatically. That's not the case! Gardeners need to inspect their sprinkler system as least weekly to make sure it's performing well; that nozzles are in adjustment and that heads are able to reach their intended target. It's also important to monitor the season and the weather and adjust the system to match any natural precipitation the lawn receives.

Sprinkler system performance. The design, maintenance, and management of your sprinkler system directly influence the quality of your lawn and the amount of water you can conserve. In fact, overwatering is the most common problem associated with automatic sprinkler systems. If you want to reduce water usage in your landscape, evaluate the condition of your sprinkler system.

You can hire a professional to conduct a comprehensive irrigation audit or you can conduct a basic system check. Here is a sample sprinkler system checklist:

- Identify site problems (slope and sun exposure).
- Identify soil problems (soil type).
- Inspect the entire system for needed repairs (check sprinkler heads, valves, etc.).
- Determine precipitation rates with catch cans or a similar method.
- Determine uniformity of each zone (how evenly the water infiltrates each zone).
- Determine if all sprinkler heads are the same type.
- Determine if sprinkler spray heads are properly adjusted to water the lawn (not sidewalks, driveways, and pavement).
- Determine if all areas are receiving adequate water.
- Determine if sprinkler heads are properly spaced.
- Determine if any sprinkler heads need replacing.
- Check water pressure (too high or too low).
- Check for leaking valves.

Did you find any areas for improvement? Then take the appropriate steps to bring your system into top working order.

Water management practices. When Denver Water imposed mandatory watering restrictions in 2004, I was probably one of the few people who liked being told when I could water my lawn. It took the guesswork out of watering. I knew that I could water on Monday, Wednesday, and Saturday between 6:00 P.M. and 10:00

A.M. I knew that I could only water each zone for twenty minutes. The schedule dictated when I watered and how much I could water my lawn.

I didn't have to ask questions like: "What is my soil's ability to hold water and make it available to my lawn?" or "How much water is being lost through evaporation and turfgrass transpiration?" I didn't have to ponder, "How deep are my lawn's roots?"

These questions reflect the type of factors to consider when determining a lawn-watering schedule. For example, lawns that grow in amended soils have the capacity to store more water and encourage deeper turfgrass roots. Deeper roots allow the plant to take up more nutrients and water, which results in needing fewer watering days. Lawns grown on sandy soil, where water quickly seeps through, have less water-storage capacity. If the grass doesn't receive enough nutrients and water, the roots may stay near the soil surface, where they're more likely to dry out during hot weather.

To make the most of your sprinkler system, don't set the schedule in the spring and walk away. Plan on adapting your irrigation schedule during the course of the season. Pay attention to your lawn's water needs and to changes in the weather so you can prevent overwatering. In fact, your lawn will actually tell you when it's thirsty. When the grass starts to change color from darker green to lighter green and when you can see your footprints in the lawn, add water. A rain gauge is also a handy tool to measure the amount of water your turf is receiving.

Use the Soak Cycle

Irrigation management is now a priority everywhere in Colorado. One way to make the most of your watering schedule is to water half the allotted time per zone and then wait for the water to soak into the soil (about thirty to sixty minutes). Then water the remaining time. This method allows for deeper irrigation and minimizes runoff due to dry soils.

ET controllers. Using an evapotranspiration (ET) controller with your sprinkler system is another way to schedule irrigation. ET is the combination of water that evaporates from the soil and the water that's lost through transpiration from plants. An ET controller uses information it receives from on-site sensors and/or weather stations to set daily irrigation run-time schedules. The controller is used to increase or decrease the schedule according to changes in the weather. This conserves water. For example, if your area receives rain, the ET data can save you a number of irrigations based on the lawn's water use and available soil moisture.

ET data, whether historical or real time, help gardeners calculate and adjust the timing of their lawn irrigation. Historical data are available from your water provider to help you adjust your controllers each month.

> ## Create an Irrigation Schedule
>
> An irrigation scheduler is available at www.water saver.org. This Web site lets you create a run-time scheduler to customize an irrigation schedule to individual landscapes and irrigation systems in metro Denver, Colorado Springs, Fort Collins, and Grand Junction.

Real-time ET, either by a fixed-day method or a fixed-amount method, is used to determine how much water to apply during each watering session. Computerized irrigation managers are used commercially and will soon be available to the home gardener. For information on how to use an ET controller with your sprinkler system, see www.coloradoet.org.

Turf Renovation

If your lawn used to be thick and healthy but now seems less vigorous, it may need a little rejuvenating through renovation.

Topdressing. Applying a thin layer of topdressing, like compost or other organic matter, helps improve the quality of the soil on mature lawns. Apply it about 1 inch deep over the entire lawn and rake in. Topdressing is usually done after aerating to help improve water absorption. I used topdressing to repair a bad spot in the front lawn. One area always looked worse than the rest of the yard and dried out more quickly than other parts of the lawn. I added a little compost to the area about once a week and spot watered it when it looked dry. In just a few weeks, the spot had filled in and started to look as nice as the rest of the lawn.

Overseeding is a another way to rejuvenate a lawn and increase grass density. Mature lawns—as well as those thinned by dry winters, dog traffic, or pests—can benefit from overseeding. If you want to overseed your established lawn, spring is the time to do it, especially in combination with aerating the lawn. The core holes create a perfect environment for germinating grass seed. Remember that preemergent herbicides shouldn't be used if you're planning to overseed.

Turfgrass Problems

Turfgrass that is thin, drought-stressed, or dog damaged is more susceptible to weeds, lawn pests, and diseases. Many of these

problems have similar symptoms: Dry yellowing patches in the grass, for instance, could be the result of mite damage or winterkill or a combination of both. It's best to be sure of the cause of turfgrass problems before taking action.

For example, when grass fails to green up in spring, most gardeners apply extra water to help it along. However, overwatering can stress the lawn even further and cause *Ascochyta* leaf blight. The lawn will eventually recover if the elements of good lawn care—core cultivation, fertilizing, appropriate watering, and mowing—are put into practice.

Weeds, pests, and diseases are some of the common causes of turfgrass problems, but not the only causes. Problems can be result from inappropriate use of pesticides, herbicides, salts, and chemicals.

Weeds

A number of common weeds cause problems in turfgrass:

- Broadleaf weeds, like dandelion, clover, thistle, and bindweed
- Weedy grasses like crabgrass and foxtail
- Perennial weedy grasses like bent grass and quack grass

Solutions for these weeds include applying a preemergent herbicide in early spring, usually before the middle of April, to prevent grassy-type weeds like crabgrass. To prevent damage to the turf, follow label applications and apply uniformly and at the suggested rate. Apply herbicides in fall to control weeds like dandelions.

Lawn Pests

There are two kinds of lawn pests in Colorado: those that are found on grass blades, like sodworms, cutworms, and turfgrass mites; and those that are found in the soil, like white grubs and bill bugs. These pests cause lawns to become thin or fail to green up in the spring. Growing a healthy lawn is key to preventing these insect pests.

Mites can cause damage to lawns that won't be noticeable until the grass begins to turn green in spring. Mite damage causes turf to turn straw yellow and can be seen in large and small patches. Mite damage looks similar to symptoms of a drought-stressed lawn, but look closely: Yellow speckles or streaks on the grass blades indicate the presence of mites. The best way to prevent mite damage is to water turf during the dry winter months.

Lawn Diseases

Diseases usually strike when lawns are under stress. Practicing good lawn practices—like aerating, watering, and fertilizing—can solve many of the following lawn problems:

Ascochyta **leaf blight** is caused by stressors like dry soil conditions followed by wet soil conditions. It looks like a pinched, straw-colored tip on a green grass blade. The best preventive measures are monitoring the amount of irrigation and applying water in the appropriate amounts at the appropriate time for your lawn conditions.

Necrotic ring spot is a problem in Kentucky bluegrass lawns. This turf disease shows up as patches of live grass within a circle of dead grass. Basic turf management practices include moderate fertilizing, aerating, correct watering practices, and mowing the lawn at 2½ to 3 inches in height.

Leaf spot and melting out diseases are caused by fungi. These diseases show up as black or dark spots on the grass leaf blade. Good lawn practices are the best controls.

Dollar spot is also caused by a fungus. It is often confused with *Ascochyta* because the appearance is similar. Proper lawn maintenance practices can help control dollar spot.

Most cooperative extension offices can help you identify turf-grass problems. Contact your county's office for information on the procedure for taking a turf sample.

Invasive Plants

Just because a plant looks lovely in the landscape, it doesn't necessarily belong there. Here's a story illustrating that point: While taking a tour of model homes in a new housing development in northern Colorado, a gardener stopped to admire the attractive landscaping in front of one of the homes. The showy bright purple flowers on the tall plant caught her eye. On closer inspection she was shocked to see that it was a purple loosestrife. Purple loosestrife (*Lythrum salicaria*) has been referred to as "public enemy number one" on public lands in over half the states in the country.

Purple loosestrife is almost indestructible. This escaped ornamental grows in marshes and in wetlands near lakes, rivers, and streams. When it takes over it threatens the natural habitat of waterfowl and wildlife. It's designated a noxious weed in our state and targeted for eradication. Obviously it shouldn't be used in any landscaping design.

Weeds in the backyard can be annoying. Certainly they're aggravating. But usually they're harmless. A patch of crabgrass in the backyard will take some work to eliminate, but it won't cause problems for anyone but the home owner. That's when a weed is just a weed.

But sometimes a weed becomes such a pest that it upsets the balance of a natural environment. These weeds act like aliens from another planet. They are aggressive, spread quickly, and defy our best attempts to eradicate them. Some started out as nice ornamental plants, but now they've jumped the garden gate and have spread into natural areas.

Invasive plants are a big problem in Colorado. At least one million acres of land have been contaminated by them. These invaders have a negative effect on all of us who love the natural beauty of our state. This chapter explains the nature of invasive plants, why they're a problem, and what we, as gardeners, can do to prevent the spread of these invaders.

Defining the Problem

Many sources credit Luther Burbank with the saying, "A weed is any plant growing in the wrong place." But invasive plants are more than just weeds. To avoid confusion when discussing invasive plants, it's helpful to define some key terms:

Native species are plants that grow naturally in a particular region and are an essential part of the landscape. They are well adapted to survive weather extremes, and they provide food and shelter for wildlife.

Nonnative species (also referred to as introduced species, exotic species, or alien species) are plants that were transported from outside the United States and introduced into our area either intentionally or accidentally. Most nonnative species aren't problem plants. In fact, many are harmless and useful.

Invasive species are nonnative species that have the ability to quickly and aggressively spread and disrupt an ecosystem.

Invasive species cause substantial damage to the environment or economy.

A *weed* is a plant that is invasive and alien to the surrounding ecosystem.

Noxious weed is a nonnative species that aggressively invades an area and causes agricultural or environmental damage. It is listed by a federal, state, county, or local agency for eradication or management. A plant may be classified as a noxious weed in one state and not in others.

Invasive ornamental plants (also called escaped ornamentals) are nonnative plants that were originally planted in gardens and have escaped into native plant communities. The characteristics that once made them ideal garden plants cause problems once they spread into other environments. They grow aggressively, spread easily, and have few natural enemies. Kudzu is one example of a plant that was brought in to control soil erosion but is now a noxious weed in the South.

Most plants stay where they're planted, but many are able to roam. Birds and small mammals disperse seeds and berries; wind and rain runoff also send seeds on their way. When invasive plants move in, native plants are forced out, causing a chain reaction in the

The Tamarisk Problem

Tamarisk (salt cedar) is a nonnative species that is causing extreme harm to wetlands and riparian areas throughout Colorado and the Southwest. This woody shrub has pushed out native cottonwoods, reduced native plants and biodiversity, and reduced bird and wildlife habitat. It uses millions of acre-feet of water each year and is extremely difficult to eradicate. Colorado is currently working on a ten-year plan for tamarisk control. For updates on the tamarisk control plan, see the Colorado Department of Natural Resources Web site (www.dnr.state.co.us).

environment. Without native vegetation, insects, birds, and other wildlife suffer; the loss of habitat causes plant and wildlife species to become endangered or threatened. Reduced biodiversity can alter an area forever. Changes in vegetation can also lead to increased soil erosion, more frequent fires, and negatively affect ranching and farming, property values, watersheds, recreational opportunities, and health (human and animal).

The View from Southern Colorado

Whenever a road is graded, a trail is built, or land is cleared for a housing development, native plants are displaced—making room for opportunistic invasive plants. "This has a big impact on real estate and income in our valley," says Christina MacLeod of Westcliffe. "Canada thistle loves this environment and goes to seed before many of our native plants. It takes at least five years of sustained effort, including mowing and using chemicals, to eradicate it once it starts spreading."

MacLeod is a native plant expert, a weed specialist, and an environmental educator. In 2001 she purchased thirty-five acres of land in southern Colorado with the intent to reclaim the original landscape and preserve the diversity of native plants in that area. "Part of my mission as an environmental educator is to bring a heightened consciousness of the richness and diversity of the plants we've inherited and to demonstrate the value of that," she says. Part of her mission includes managing weeds.

MacLeod is active on the Custer County Weed Advisory Board, which supports the county extension office's efforts to assist landowners in managing invasive plants and noxious weeds in the county. She also works with the Custer County Conservation District Board of Supervisors, part of a state- and nationwide network of county boards that promotes the responsible use, practice, and management of the county's natural resources, with a priority on farming and ranching.

"My observation is that invasives get a foothold almost entirely because of humans. Disturbance to the soil or ecosystem makes an area vulnerable. For example, overgrazing is what makes a hay meadow vulnerable and weakens its ability to compete with aggressive weeds. Other evidence of the human footprint can be anything from footpaths to four-wheel roads to horse trails," she explains.

It requires time, energy, and money to eradicate established weed populations. "Weed infestation reduces available grazing land because weeds outcompete the native vegetation and grasses. This also causes a loss of habitat for wildlife. They'll migrate elsewhere to find what they need. Pushing out natives results in both plant and animal species endangerment or loss," MacLeod says.

MacLeod recommends that all gardeners, especially those who are new to our state, learn about our invasive plants. "Learn which weeds are most problematic in your area and what others are doing to solve the problem. If weeds are a problem on your land, meet with your county extension director and learn what resources are available for weed management," she recommends. And learn how to identify weeds and the best ways for managing them, whether by hand pulling, a mowing schedule, or chemical options.

Above all, "if you find that something you have planted is becoming invasive, take steps to manage it; certainly don't let it go to seed."

Colorado's Top-Five Invasive Plant Issues

Eric Lane, the state weed coordinator, explains that Colorado has at least five pressing issues when it comes to invasive plants.

Issue #1—Keep new invasive plants out of Colorado. New plant species arrive every year, introduced accidentally or purposefully for a variety of reasons. There are many invasive plants/noxious weeds across the West, but they aren't uniformly distributed. Some species, like leafy spurge and diffuse knapweed, are well established in parts of Colorado but are rare in California and Arizona. Conversely, some species that are common in other western states are moving toward Colorado, spread by wind, water, wildlife, and people. In recent years yellow star thistle, African rue, and Mediterranean sage have been introduced unintentionally in Colorado. Other species have been brought in purposefully, perhaps for ornamental or medicinal value. "The recent discovery of an infestation of dyer's woad in the city of Boulder can likely trace its introduction to someone who imported the plant (probably from Utah) for its use as a natural plant dye," says Lane.

Gardeners have contributed to the problem, says Lane. "Unfortunately, many of the characteristics that gardeners seek in a plant—like drought tolerance, high seed production, and persistence—are also characteristics of invasive plants." Some gardeners unintentionally or sometimes purposely introduce these problems to their communities; other times people fail to respond quickly once they learn they have a problem plant. "Some can't believe their beautiful purple loosestrife or oxeye daisy plant has spread and become a problem. With so many other beautiful and noninvasive plants to cultivate, it's irresponsible to allow known invasive plants to spread to other properties, community open space, and public land," he says. "We need to prevent the accidental and intentional introduction of additional species of invasive plants."

Issue #2—Detect and eradicate new invaders quickly. Prevention is important, but new invasive species will slip in despite our best efforts, Lane says. "We must be able to identify new introductions quickly and eradicate them before they can become established." The key here is developing more "trained eyes" in communities across Colorado—local gardeners who can "identify new invaders and report them promptly to local noxious weed management programs." You can find list of county weed supervisors at www.ag.state.co.us.

Issue #3—Develop and implement plans for managing well-established species. Numerous species of invasive plants are already well established in Colorado. "Early detection and eradication is no longer a strategy we can rely upon to address species like leafy spurge and Russian knapweed," he notes. As abundant as these invasive plants may be in some parts of Colorado, Lane says, it's still possible to stop the invaders in those Colorado communities where the plants are just becoming established.

Issue #4—Identify areas for protection. "Many areas of Colorado are still uninfested by noxious weeds and retain their beauty and values as wildlands and working farms and ranches," Lane says. He advocates the concept of "weed prevention areas" in which key areas are identified and serious efforts are made to protect high-value areas from future invasions.

Issue #5—Cultivate a greater stewardship ethic. "While there are many landowners who take great pride in protecting their land from invasive plants, there are many more who are unaware of the impact of noxious weeds," Lane states. "All landowners have a responsibility to manage noxious weeds on their properties so that these species cannot spread. In Colorado, we must cultivate a greater stewardship ethic so that all landowners understand that with land comes responsibility to protect the values of land."

How You Can Help

Eric Lane identifies six ways that gardeners can help solve the problem of invasive weeds:

1. Start at home. Review what's growing in your garden to ensure there are no "felons." Commonly planted invasive ornamentals in Colorado include:
   - Bouncing bet (*Saponaria officinalis*)
   - Chinese clematis (*Clematis orientalis*)
   - Common Saint-John's-wort (*Hypericum perforatum*)
   - Common tansy (*Tanacetum vulgare*)
   - Cypress spurge (*Euphorbia cyparissias*)
   - Dame's rocket (*Hesperis matronalis*)
   - Myrtle spurge (*Euphorbia myrsinites*)
   - Orange hawkweed (*Hieracium aurantiacum*)
   - Oxeye daisy (*Chrysanthemum leucanthemum*)
   - Purple loosestrife (*Lythrum salicaria* and *L. virgatum*)

More Ways to Stop Invasives

Here are additional ways Colorado gardeners can help prevent ornamental invasive plants from becoming a problem:

- Buy and plant natives; ask nurseries to carry native plants.
- Learn how to recognize invasive ornamentals in their different stages of development.
- Read labels carefully on wildflower or grass seed mixes and don't plant if the contents aren't clearly described or if the mix contains prohibited ornamentals.
- When ordering plants from a catalog or Web site, be sure the plant isn't one known to be a regionally invasive species.
- Know what plants are listed on Colorado's noxious weed lists.
- Replace invasive ornamentals with ornamentals known to be noninvasive.

- Russian olive (*Elaeagnus angustifolia*)
- Salt cedar (*Tamarix chinensis, T. parviflora,* and *T. ramosissima*)
- Scentless chamomile (*Matricaria perforatum*)
- Yellow toadflax (*Linaria vulgaris*)

2. Remove invasive ornamentals and dispose of them. Double-bag the plants and put them out for trash removal or take them to the local landfill.

3. Remain vigilant for any reappearance. Plants may grow back from remaining rootstock or seed.

4. Check around the neighborhood to make sure invasive plants haven't escaped to neighboring properties and open spaces.

5. Identify invasive plant problems and contact the local weed management program (county or municipal).

6. Educate others. Too many gardeners fail to take this issue seriously. Speak out about the issue and how gardeners can help.

When a Daisy Goes Bad

Here is a list of invasive ornamental plants that Colorado gardeners should avoid. The alternatives will provide some of the same characteristics but won't cause environmental damage.

- **Dame's rocket** (*Hesperis matronalis*). Alternatives: Colorado columbine (*Aquilegia caerula*), lavender native bee balm (*Monarda fistula* var. *menthaefolia*)

- **Oxeye daisy** (*Chrysantheum leucanthemum*). Alternatives: native daisies (*Erigeron* spp.), black-eyed Susan (*Rudbeckia hirta*), blanketflower (*Gaillardia aristata*)

- **Scentless chamomile** (*Matricaria perforata*). Alternatives: Feverfew (*Tanacetum parthenium*), cutleaf daisy (*Erigeron compostitus*), native daises (*Erigeron* spp.)

- **Myrtle spurge** (*Euphorbia myrsinites*). Alternatives: sulphur flower (*Erigonum umbellatum*), kinnikinnik (*Artcostaphylos uva-ursi*)

- **Russian olive** (*Elaeagnus angustifolia*). Alternatives: cottonwood (*Populus deltoides* or *P. angustifolia*), chokecherry (*Prunus virginiana*), silverleaf buffaloberry (*Shepherdia argentea*)

- **Dalmatian toadflax and yellow toadflax** (*Linaria genistifolia* ssp. *dalmatica* and *L. vulgaris*). Alternatives: Snapdragons (*Antirrhinum* spp.)

Colorado Noxious Weeds

Invasive plants are rated based on the harmful effects they have on natural environments, native plant habitats, and agriculture. According to state weed coordinator Eric Lane, there are two steps to the rating:

1. The plant is designated as a noxious weed. This means it is nonnative, is aggressively invasive, and causes agricultural or environmental harm.

2. The noxious weed is then classified into List A, B, or C. This classification is based upon the species' known distribution, the feasibility of control with the current technology, and the cost to implement a statewide management plan.

Lane explains that List A noxious weeds are slated for statewide eradication because they have a limited distribution, can be controlled effectively with current technology, and the cost to implement a statewide management plan is reasonable. While statewide eradication is no longer feasible for more widespread List B species, efforts are made to stop their continued spread throughout the state. Because List C species are so widespread that halting their continued spread is no longer possible, there is no statewide coordinated management effort, but attempts are made to help communities improve the management of these noxious weeds.

Colorado's List A noxious weeds:

- African rue (*Peganum harmala*)
- Camelthorn (*Alhagi pseudalhagi*)
- Common crupina (*Crupina vulgaris*)
- Cypress spurge (*Euphorbia cyparissias*)
- Dyer's woad (*Isatis tinctoria*)
- Giant salvinia (*Salvinia molesta*)
- Hydrilla (*Hydrilla verticillata*)

- Meadow knapweed (*Centaurea pratensis*)
- Mediterranean sage (*Salvia aethiopis*)
- Medusahead (*Taeniatherum caput-medusae*)
- Myrtle spurge (*Euphorbia myrsinites*)
- Orange hawkweed (*Hieracium aurantiacum*)
- Purple loosestrife (*Lythrum salicaria*)
- Rush skeletonweed (*Chondrilla juncea*)
- Sericea lespedeza (*Lespedeza cuneata*)
- Squarrose knapweed (*Centaurea virgata*)
- Tansy ragwort (*Senecio jacobaea*)
- Yellow star thistle (*Centaurea solstitialis*)

Colorado's List B noxious weeds:

- Absinth wormwood (*Artemisia absinthium*)
- Black henbane (*Hyoscyamus niger*)
- Bouncing bet (*Saponaria officinalis*)
- Bull thistle (*Cirsium vulgare*)
- Canada thistle (*Cirsium arvense*)
- Chinese clematis (*Clematis orientalis*)
- Common tansy (*Tanacetum vulgare*)
- Common teasel (*Dipsacus fullonum*)
- Corn chamomile (*Anthemis arvensis*)
- Cutleaf teasel (*Dipsacus laciniatus*)
- Dalmatian toadflax, broad-leaved (*Linaria dalmatica*)
- Dalmatian toadflax, narrow-leaved (*Linaria genistifolia*)
- Dame's rocket (*Hesperis matronalis*)

- Diffuse knapweed (*Centaurea diffusa*)

- Eurasian watermilfoil (*Myriophyllum spicatum*)

- Hoary cress (*Cardaria draba*)

- Houndstongue (*Cynoglossum officinale*)

- Leafy spurge (*Euphorbia esula*)

- Mayweed chamomile (*Anthemis cotula*)

- Moth mullein (*Verbascum blattaria*)

- Musk thistle (*Carduus nutans*)

- Oxeye daisy (*Chrysanthemum leucanthemum*)

- Perennial pepperweed (*Lepidium latifolium*)

- Plumeless thistle (*Carduus acanthoides*)

- Quack grass (*Elytrigia repens*)

- Redstem filaree (*Erodium cicutarium*)

- Russian knapweed (*Acroptilon repens*)

- Russian olive (*Elaeagnus angustifolia*)

- Salt cedar (*Tamarix chinensis, T. parviflora,* and *T. ramosissima*)

- Scentless chamomile (*Matricaria perforata*)

- Scotch thistle (*Onopordum acanthium* and *O. tauricum*)

- Spotted knapweed (*Centaurea maculosa*)

- Spurred anoda (*Anoda cristata*)

- Sulfur cinquefoil (*Potentilla recta*)

- Venice mallow (*Hibiscus trionum*)

- Wild caraway (*Carum carvi*)

- Yellow nutsedge (*Cyperus esculentus*)

- Yellow toadflax (*Linaria vulgaris*)

Colorado's List C noxious weeds:

- Chicory (*Cichorium intybus*)

- Common burdock (*Arctium minus*)

- Common mullein (*Verbascum thapsus*)

- Common Saint-John's-wort (*Hypericum perforatum*)

- Downy brome (*Bromus tectorum*)

- Field bindweed (*Convolvulus arvensis*)

- Halogeton (*Halogeton glomeratus*)

- Johnsongrass (*Sorghum halepense*)

- Jointed goatgrass (*Aegilops cylindrica*)

- Perennial sowthistle (*Sonchus arvensis*)

- Poison hemlock (*Conium maculatum*)

- Puncturevine (*Tribulus terrestris*)

- Velvetleaf (*Abutilon theophrasti*)

- Wild proso millet (*Panicum miliaceum*)

Another Good Reason to Know Your Weeds

A group of Denver master gardeners at a local farmer's market was asked to identify a plant sample. The sample's owner said the plant grew in his yard, looked like a bushy shrub, and had little berries that were tasty to eat.

The group of four master gardeners crowded together and closely examined the plant. No one recognized it. A copy of the *Identification Key for Woody Plants in the Pikes Peak Region* was consulted and questions were asked. "Did it have simple leaves or compound leaves?" "Were the leaves opposite or alternate?" "Were there thorns or was it thornless?"

Because the sample didn't fit the profile of any woody plant, all the answers led to a dead end. There was much more discussion, but the group was no closer to identifying the sample. One master gardener swallowed her pride and took part of the sample to a nurseryman at a nearby table. He recognized it immediately. "That's nightshade," he said.

Nightshade is a poisonous plant. No one should be eating those berries, no matter how tasty they are.

Garden
Solutions

Coping with Pests and Diseases

Are you the kind of gardener who wages chemical warfare the moment you see an insect in your yard? Or maybe you're an organic gardener, the kind who only uses natural pesticides or none at all.

I've never used many chemicals in the yard, but I'm not a strict organic gardener, either. I choose my pest battles carefully. The only time I bring out chemical pesticides is when I see a black widow spider building a web near the house or wasps building a nest in the garden shed.

Not every insect is a pest and not every pest is an insect. But prevention is the key to avoiding pest problems in the first place.

This chapter provides a perspective for managing insect pests called integrated pest management (IPM). We'll also look at common plant diseases and their symptoms and possible causes, and discuss ways of encouraging beneficial insects to join you in your garden.

Seven Practices in the IPM System

IPM is a commonsense approach to deciding how to deal with pests in your garden. The goal is to manage pests by increasing the use of natural processes to reduce pest populations and decreasing the use of synthetic chemical pesticides. It's a system of three pest control tactics: biological, cultural, and chemical. IPM advocates selecting the most environmentally friendly method first. Natural or synthetic pesticides are used only when other methods have failed.

"Sometimes a nonchemical method of controlling pests is as effective and convenient as a chemical alternative," says the Environmental Protection Agency. The seven practices of the IPM system help gardeners make smarter choices when it comes to controlling pests. The practices include:

1. Set an acceptable level of pests. Decide how many pests you can deal with before you need to take control measures. When that level is reached, apply the most environmentally friendly and least toxic control.

2. Use good cultural practices. Selecting disease-resistant plant varieties is a preventive method. Growing healthy plants and lawns, conducting regular maintenance, and irrigating properly are all preventive cultural practices. Other methods include disposing of diseased plants and rotating vegetable crops in the garden.

3. Inspect plants regularly. Careful observation is a key IPM practice. When you spot the early stages of a problem, decide if you want to take action. For example, if the damage is only cosmetic, you may want to delay action to see what happens. Weigh the cost of chemicals with the kind of damage that's being done. If the damage will be serious, you'll want to take action immediately.

4. Apply physical and mechanical controls. These controls are implemented when an unacceptable pest level is reached. For example, you can handpick insects from plants, set insect barriers, use traps, or spray with water.

5. Use biological controls. Predators, parasites, and pathogens are three biological controls for pests. Natural enemies can target specific insect pests and reduce their populations. Beneficial insects include lady beetles (ladybugs), lacewing larvae, and spiders. Birds are also welcome insect predators.

6. Apply biological insecticides. These living organisms (or the toxins produced by them) include viruses, bacteria, fungi, and nematodes. These natural insecticides cause death in targeted pests. For example, *Bacillus thuringiensis* (Bt) is a naturally occurring soil bacterium that causes disease in certain insects.

7. Use chemical methods. There are two kinds of chemical methods: biorationals and synthetics. Try the least toxic chemical controls first, like diatomaceous earth. This powder causes insects to dehydrate and die. Other chemicals include insecticidal soaps, oils, repellents, boric acid, and borate. Conventional pesticides are synthetic pesticides that kill insects on contact. These should be used only when all other controls fail. Conventional pesticides kill beneficial insects as well as the insect pests.

Think of these IPM practices as steps on a ladder. Always start at the bottom of the ladder with preventive and cultural methods. Because each rung of the ladder involves a higher degree of intervention, use the least toxic measures first. You bring out the heavy artillery—the chemical controls—only after all of the other methods have been tried and found to be ineffective. IPM is designed to minimize long-term, harmful environmental effects and health hazards.

What's Bugging You in the Garden?

Insects are most decidedly pests in the garden, but there are other pests that are just as annoying. Here are some of our most common garden pests:

Landscape weeds
- Crabgrass
- Dandelion
- Chickweed
- Clover
- Purslane
- Bindweed
- Puncturevine

Plant diseases
- *Ascochta* leaf blight
- Necrotic ring spot
- Fire blight
- Powdery mildew
- Bacterial blight
- Bacterial leaf spot
- Rose diseases
- Tomato diseases

Insect pests
- Aphids
- Codling moth
- Mites
- Beetles
- Grasshoppers

- Psyllids
- Squash bug
- Turf mites
- Tent caterpillars
- Leafhoppers
- Thrips

Vertebrates
- Squirrels
- Rabbits
- Deer
- Mice
- Raccoons
- Voles

Sometimes gardeners are their own enemy, too. Over-watering is one of the most common plant health issues.

To Your Plant's Good Health

Growing healthy plants is what gardening is all about. It's a combination of matching the plant to the right site and giving it the proper amounts of nutrients, water, and sunlight. Not only are healthy plants more beautiful, they produce more crops. And plants that are healthy are better able to resist an insect onslaught or disease.

Plants can suffer ill health for a number of reasons:

- They can be predisposed to problems because of poor cultural practices, like not properly preparing the soil prior to planting or when soils are overwatered, causing roots to rot.

- They can become stressed due to inciting environmental factors, such as a prolonged drought.

- They can suffer from a combination of problems. For example, insects may attack a plant that is stressed due to combination of environmental and cultural practices.

A plant's needs change throughout its lifecycle. For example, a tree has different needs when it's being grown in the nursery, when it's becoming established in your yard, when it's actively growing, and when it's mature. Providing the right kind of care at the right time helps ensure the health of your plants.

Diagnosing Plant Health Problems

Colorado gardeners are fortunate because plant diseases are less common here than in wetter climates. The low rates of precipitation and humidity make conditions less hospitable for diseases to flourish.

Usually it's easy to tell when a plant isn't feeling well. It may wilt or be stunted in growth; leaves may drop, curl, or turn yellow. Plant problems develop because three factors are in play: a disease-causing organism (often called a pathogen) is present, the plant is susceptible to that pathogen, and the environment creates perfect conditions for diseases to develop. Together these are known as the disease triangle. All three factors must be present for a disease to occur. Remove (control) one factor and you have a good shot at curtailing disease.

Plant diseases are classified as either biotic (living causes like insects, fungi, bacteria, and viruses) or abiotic (nonliving causes related to soil, weather, and cultural practices). The majority of plant disease problems in Colorado fall into the abiotic category.

Here are the basic steps to identifying plant health problems:

- Know your plant. Accurate identification of the plant, and knowing what it looks like when it's healthy, assists in identifying the insect or disease. Many problems are plant specific, so accurate identification narrows the universe of potential problems.

- Give the plant a checkup. Examine the leaves, stems, trunk, and the area where the plant is growing. Check the roots if possible.
  - ✓ Are leaves mottled, crinkled, or stunted?
  - ✓ Are there leaf blights, spots, abnormal growths, or rotted roots?

The Mountain Pine Beetle

There are pests and then there are *real* pests, like the mountain pine beetle. The scope of this pest's devastation is hard to fathom—infestations of these beetles have caused extensive damage to forests filled with lodgepole and ponderosa pine trees in Grand, Routt, and Summit Counties, where these trees were in a weakened condition because of drought. Spraying with liquid insecticides may help prevent beetle infestations in susceptible pine trees. This is an important method for keeping a hazardous pest from destroying entire forests. Bark beetles can also attack pine trees along the Front Range. If you have large pine trees in your yard, you may want to consider preventive spraying. Contact an experienced arborist for specific recommendations.

✓ Are the leaves curled, spotted, or wilted? Are there abnormal swellings or sunken areas?

✓ Do the leaves or needles look burned: Are leaves yellow, do they drop prematurely, or are they smaller than normal?

• Determine if the damage follows a pattern. If the injury is uniform, then environmental factors could be responsible; random injury means living organisms could be the cause.

Plant Problem Symptoms and Causes

The following list outlines some common plant symptoms and possible causes. Plant problems can have similar symptoms, but different causes. It's important to accurately identify the problem before taking steps to control it. Controls can be effective only if the problem is correctly identified and the correct solution applied.

Once you've identified the plant and narrowed down the symptom(s) and possible cause(s), you can do a little research to confirm your diagnosis and then provide appropriate treatment. Or you can take a sample to a plant diagnostic clinic, designed to diagnose both insect and disease problems, provided through CSU Cooperative Extension offices throughout the state. Contact your county office for information.

Symptom	Possible cause
Chewed leaves, abnormal swelling (galls), skeletonized leaf, leaf distortion, yellowing of leaves, webbing on underside of leaves.	Insect damage (caterpillars, beetles, grasshoppers)
Leaves have mosaic pattern, yellow and green mottled pattern, stunted growth, deformed or distorted leaves and flowers.	Viruses (for example, rose mosaic virus, tomato spot wilt virus)

Symptom	Possible cause
Leaf spots, abnormal swelling (galls), soft rots, sunken areas (cankers), wilts; slimy, shiny, water-soaked texture; translucent spots.	Bacteria (like fire blight)
Leaf spots, curling, abnormal swelling, wilts, sunken areas (cankers), stem and root rots, seedlings come up but flop over (damping off), leaf coated with white powdery material, dry areas, fluffy areas.	Fungi (like powdery mildew, rusts)
Blackened tips of leaves, yellowing, leaf scorch, wilting, leaf drop, leaf distortion, spotting.	Abiotic problem such as overwatering, poor soil drainage, freezing temperatures, nutrient deficiencies, herbicide use, drought

Beneficial Insects

Keep in mind that some insect damage may be caused by beneficial insects instead of pests. For example, native leaf-cutter bees take circular snippets out of rose leaves to line their nests for young bees. Because that damage doesn't hurt the roses, gardeners should refrain from applying chemical controls. On the other hand, pests like the rose midge may deserve a shot or two. They prevent roses from blooming.

Colorado gardeners are lucky when it comes to insect pests. We have fewer problems than gardeners in more humid climates, and Colorado ranks in the bottom percentile of bugs. The state is home to at least seven kinds of ants and many more species of spiders and other beneficial insects. However, each summer gardeners feel they need to wage war against these tiny insects.

Ants

"What's the harm of ants?" asks Whitney Cranshaw, CSU professor of entomology and author of *Garden Insects of North America: The Ultimate Guide to Backyard Bugs* and *Pests of the West.* "Eliminating ants is a pointless exercise. You can eliminate the colony, but they will come back."

Ants may be a nuisance, but they're not considered garden pests. Ants offer gardeners more positives than negatives, especially when it comes to protecting plants from the real pests. Ants in lawns are busy eating other insects, which means fewer lawn problems, says Cranshaw.

Besides being some of the world's most important insect predators, ants disperse seeds and aerate the soil. Ants are expert earthmovers that can move more dirt than earthworms. Sometimes their nest building may cause plant damage when their tunneling disturbs the soil around roots. But the damage gardeners see on plants is usually due to aphids, not ants. Ants protect aphids from other predators because ants want the sweet honeydew that aphids secrete.

The only time Cranshaw takes measures to control ants in his yard is when he sees damage on plants caused by aphids. "The ants defend aphids against their natural enemies, like the lady beetle," he says.

Ants may signal an aphid problem, but ants tending their aphid flocks aren't a big deal in the total picture, he says. "If it bothers you because of your aesthetic sense, you can try to control ants, but you can't eliminate them."

Cranshaw says that if ants were eliminated completely, the ecosystem would collapse. "Basically just leave ants alone," he advises. "They have little impact on us and you're not going to get rid of ants. Your efforts are for naught."

Spiders

Despite their reputation as loathsome creatures, spiders are one of the landscape's best friends. We might be up to our knees in pests if it weren't for our eight-legged helpers. "Without spiders in the garden, there'd be more insects eating plants. Spiders are nature's way of keeping a check on the insect population," says Paula Cushing, curator of invertebrate zoology at the Denver Museum of Nature and Science.

As beneficial predators, spiders feed on living insects, like blackflies, mosquitoes, grasshoppers, and other pests. Not all spiders spin webs to catch their prey. Some are hunters that stalk their quarry; others wait for dinner to come to them.

"Most savvy gardeners understand that it's a good thing to have spiders in the garden," says Cushing. "They have a better appreciation for spiders than the general public."

Fear of spiders ranges from the "eeek" factor to petrifying arachnophobia. This aversion may come from their daunting appearance, stories about their poisonous bites, or images lingering from movies about eight-legged radioactive monsters.

Cushing says that kind of fear is unwarranted. "There's no logical reason to be afraid of spiders. There are very few that are harmful to humans. It's a little silly to be scared of something so much smaller." Instead, spiders should be afraid of us. Indiscriminate use of pesticides presents a scary future for these creepy crawlers.

Gardeners can encourage spiders to live in their yards by taking a few simple steps. Cushing recommends planting a complex landscape, one that includes everything from low-lying plants to flowering shrubs. The variety of plants means more attachment points for webs. Mulch provides moisture and hiding places. In addition to encouraging spiders, a layered landscape also attracts insects. "The higher the numbers of insects, the higher the number of predators," Cushing explains.

Other Beneficial Insects

Predators, parasites, and pollinators are three kinds of beneficial insects in the garden. Before taking any action for controlling insect pest populations, be sure to identify the insect correctly. For example, the parsley worm is similar in size to the tomato hornworm, but it feeds on dill and parsley and then turns into the black swallowtail butterfly.

Attract beneficial insects to your yard by creating a garden environment where populations of good bugs balance with the populations of insect pests. Beneficial insects in Colorado include:

- Lady beetles (ladybugs) and their larvae
- Green lacewing larvae
- Honeybees and bumblebees
- Paper wasps
- Hoverflies
- True bugs
- Ground beetles
- Predatory mites

Birds are a good natural control for insect pests, too. To attract birds to your yard, create a backyard habitat. Grow plants (especially native perennials and shrubs) that provide food and shelter, set up a bird feeding station, and keep a birdbath full of clean water. Birds help control insect populations in the garden and in the lawn, but only if these areas are free of pesticides and herbicides.

The Good, the Bad, and the Ugly of Spiders

Colorado is home to many species of spiders, but only one is considered dangerous—the western widow spider. Its long, spindly legs and distinctive red marking on the underside of its abdomen are clear warning signs.

The most common—and beneficial—spiders in our area include:

- Funnel web spiders (Agelenidae)
- Jumping spiders (Salticidae)
- *Dysdera crocata* (wood louse hunter)
- Ground spiders (Gnaphosidae)
- Wolf spiders (Lycosidae)
- *Araneus* spiders (orb-weaving spiders)
- Banded garden spider (Araneidae)

Colorado's Spider Survey research project was started in 1999 by Paula Cushing of the Denver Museum of Nature and Science to study the distribution and diversity of spiders in our state. The project collects baseline information on a diverse group of creatures and also educates people about spiders. "The best way to increase science literacy is by getting people involved in the scientific process. By the time we're done, I expect we'll have identified between 600 and 1,000 species of spiders in Colorado," Cushing says.

Bats are also insect predators, eating thousands of flying insects each night, but it's more difficult to attract them into your yard. Bat Conservation International, based in Austin, Texas, provides information on building bat houses at www.batcon.org.

Use Pesticides Safely

The last rung on the IPM ladder is using synthetic chemical pesticides. This step is taken only when all other controls fail. Before you reach for the pesticide, remember that fewer than 10 percent of landscape pests warrant the use of pesticides. Be sure you've tried other methods first, like using a garden hose to spray off the pests (like aphids), applying an insecticidal soap, or using an organic insecticide like a neem oil derivative. You can find a variety of organic or natural pest solutions by searching the Internet.

If you must use a conventional pesticide, be sure to select the right pesticide for your specific pest need, follow all label instructions completely, spray at night when pollinators aren't active, and store or dispose of pesticides properly.

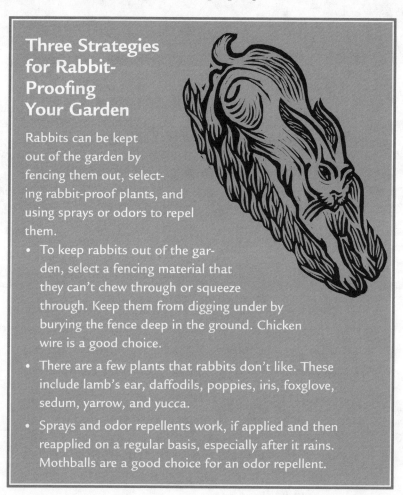

Three Strategies for Rabbit-Proofing Your Garden

Rabbits can be kept out of the garden by fencing them out, selecting rabbit-proof plants, and using sprays or odors to repel them.

- To keep rabbits out of the garden, select a fencing material that they can't chew through or squeeze through. Keep them from digging under by burying the fence deep in the ground. Chicken wire is a good choice.

- There are a few plants that rabbits don't like. These include lamb's ear, daffodils, poppies, iris, foxglove, sedum, yarrow, and yucca.

- Sprays and odor repellents work, if applied and then reapplied on a regular basis, especially after it rains. Mothballs are a good choice for an odor repellent.

Learning from Special Places

This chapter highlights some of the special plant places to visit in Colorado, gardens that teach you how to solve gardening challenges and gardens that inspire. This list is not intended to be all-inclusive, but rather a sample of the different plant environments found in our state. You'll find Xeriscape demonstration gardens, high-altitude alpine gardens, and prairie grasslands. Forgive me if I've left out your favorite garden—there are too many beautiful places to mention.

Betty Ford Alpine Gardens
183 Gore Creek Drive, Vail
(970) 476–0103
www.bettyfordalpinegardens.org
Located at 8,200 feet above sea level, this is the highest botanic garden in the world. It features a vast collection of high-elevation plants. Open daily dawn to dusk, from snowmelt to first snowfall; no admission fee. Driving directions are available on the Web site.

Butterfly Pavilion and Insect Center
6252 West 104th Avenue, Broomfield
(303) 469–5441
www.butterflies.org
An indoor tropical paradise of flowering plants provides the

perfect environment for more than 1,000 butterflies from over 250 different species. Open daily 9:00 A.M. to 5:00 P.M. in the winter; 9:00 A.M. to 6:00 P.M. Memorial Day through Labor Day. Call for admission fees.

Centennial Gardens
1101 Little Raven Street, Denver
Located in downtown Denver, near the South Platte River, this is a formal garden modeled after the gardens of Versailles, but it includes water-smart native plants. For information call Denver Botanic Gardens' information desk: (720) 865–3585.

Cheyenne Mountain Zoo
4250 Cheyenne Mountain Zoo Road, Colorado Springs
(719) 633–9925
www.cmzoo.org
Cheyenne Mountain Zoo features ten special gardens, including a Colorado Life Zones garden and a no-water garden. The zoo opens daily at 9:00 A.M.; closing time depends on the season.

Colorado State University Annual Trial Gardens
1401 Remington Street, Fort Collins
(970) 491–7019
www.flowertrials.colostate.edu
More than 1,000 varieties of annual bedding plants are evaluated at this site maintained by CSU's Department of Horticulture and Landscape Architecture.

Denver Botanic Gardens
1005 York Street, Denver
(720) 865–3500
www.botanicgardens.org
Over twenty-three acres of botanic gardens filled with plants from around the world; considered to be one of the top botanic gardens

in the nation. Call for hours, special programs, and admission information.

Denver Botanic Gardens at Chatfield
8500 Deer Creek Canyon Road, Littleton
(303) 973–3705
www.botanicgardens.org (select Location, Chatfield)
A 750-acre wildlife and native plant refuge with trails, observation areas, and gardens. Open 9:00 A.M. to 5:00 P.M. most days except major holidays.

Dushanbe Teahouse Rose Garden
1770 Thirteenth Street, Boulder
www.boulderrose.org
This is the hardy rose demonstration garden of the Boulder Valley Rose Society. Planted in 1998 the garden features fifty varieties of cold-hardy roses. The Web site details the garden's history and provides other information.

Fairmount Cemetery
430 South Quebec Street, Denver
(303) 322–3895
www.fairmountcemetery.net
The second-oldest cemetery in Denver features historic trees, sculptures, and more than 300 antique garden roses. Roses are found throughout the cemetery, including the Heritage Rose Garden near the Gazebo at Fairmount. No cuttings are allowed. A booklet on the heritage roses is available for sale at the cemetery office. Open daily dawn to dusk.

Hudson Gardens
6115 South Santa Fe Drive, Littleton
(303) 797–8565
www.hudsongardens.org

Thirty acres of gardens located along a walking path, featuring a variety of plants, flowers, and trees that thrive in Colorado. Open daily 9:00 A.M. to 5:00 P.M. Call for admission fees.

Jefferson County Sheriff's Office Public Rose Garden

200 Jefferson County Parkway, Golden

www.co.jefferson.co.us/sheriff/sheriff (search "Rose Garden")

The only public, inmate-maintained rose garden in the country; features more than 400 varieties of roses. The site is accredited through the All-American Rose Selections (AARS). The rose bowl is located on the lower west side of the complex in front of the administration building.

Mountain Park Environmental Center

9161 Mountain Park Road, Beulah

(719) 485–4444

www.hikeandlearn.org

Purchase the field guide *Plants of Pueblo Mountain Park* and hike the park's trails to see wildflowers, plants, trees, and wildlife. Call for information and special events.

Mount Goliath on the Mount Evans Scenic Byway

Clear Creek County

A high-altitude trail and interpretive site on the Mount Evans Scenic Byway. For information and reservations for wildflower hikes, call (720) 865–3577.

Plains Conservation Center

21901 East Hampden Avenue, Aurora

(303) 693–3621

www.plainscenter.org

The Plains Conservation Center depicts pioneer life in the 1880s. See plants, flowers, birds, and other animals native to the plains grasslands. Call ahead for information about special events and tours.

Plant Select Demonstration Gardens

www.plantselect.org

Nearly sixty different garden sites, located throughout the state, demonstrate the qualities of Plant Select recommendations. The Web site features a map of sites, contact information, and driving directions.

Shambhala Mountain Botanic Garden

4921 County Road 68-C,
Red Feather Lakes
(970) 881–2184
www.shambhalamountain.org

The Shambhala Botanic Gardens and Preserve is located on 700 acres at 8,000 feet. It features an organic vegetable garden, a native plant collection, a formal contemplative garden with Asian medicinal plants, and an 8-mile system of trails. Shambhala Mountain is also home to the Great Stupa of Dharmakaya, the largest example of Tibetan Buddhist sacred art in the Western Hemisphere. Open daily 9:00 A.M. to 5:00 P.M.

A Gardener's Skin Cancer Reminder

One of the advantages to gardening in Colorado is all that wonderful sunshine. However, our high altitude, combined with more than 300 days of sun each year, exposes gardeners to more ultraviolet rays than gardeners at lower elevations. Colorado gardeners need more protection from the intense sunshine. Take preventive steps to reduce the risk of skin cancer. Use ample amounts of sunscreen with an adequate SPF, wear a wide-brimmed hat and other protective clothing, and stay out of the sun from 10:00 A.M. to 2:00 P.M.

W. D. Holly Plant Environmental Research Center (PERC)

630 Lake Street, Fort Collins
(970) 491–7019
http://lamar.colostate.edu/~percgard/

Operated by the faculty and staff at the CSU's Department of

Horticulture and Landscape Architecture, PERC includes a large number of plant demonstration projects. Grounds are open to the public.

Western Colorado Botanical Gardens and Butterfly House
641 Struthers Avenue, Grand Junction
(970) 245–3288
www.wcbotanic.org
In addition to the butterfly house, the gardens include a children's secret garden, a native garden environmental education center, and a cactus and succulent garden. Open Tuesday through Sunday during its regular season. Call for dates.

Xeriscape Demonstration Gardens
www.xeriscape.org/demogardens.html
Xeriscape Colorado, a program of the Colorado WaterWise Council, lists public Xeriscape demonstration gardens throughout the state.

Yampa River Botanic Park
1000 Pamela Lane, Steamboat Springs
(970) 846–5172
www.steamboatsprings.net (Search "Yampa River Botanic Park")
Gardens feature a variety of plants that grow in a mountain environment (7,000 feet elevation), including many native flowers. The park is open dawn to dusk, spring until winter. Free admission to the public; call for wheelchair-accessible tours.

Glossary

annual: A plant that completes its lifecycle in one year.

biennial: A plant that has a two-year growth cycle.

codominant trunk: A tree that has more that one trunk of the same size; also called a codominant leader.

conifer: An evergreen, cone-bearing tree.

deciduous tree: A tree that sheds its leaves each year.

evapotranspiration (ET): The combination of water that evaporates from the soil and the water that's lost through transpiration from plants

green manure: A natural fertilizer that is grown specifically to add nutrients when tilled into the soil.

growing season: The number of days when the weather is frost free and warm enough to support planting and growing.

hardiness: An important indicator for plant survival and is dependent on geography.

hellstrip: The planting area between the sidewalk and the curb.

herbaceous perennial: A perennial plant that doesn't form woody tissue, dies to the base each year, and returns in spring.

inorganic fertilizers: Chemical fertilizers with a guaranteed amount of nutrients.

integrated pest management (IPM): A commonsense approach to dealing with insect pests; the least toxic controls are used first.

invasive ornamental: A nonnative plant that was originally planted in gardens and has escaped into the wild; also called an escaped ornamental.

invasive species: A nonnative plant species that has the ability to quickly and aggressively spread and disrupt an ecosystem.

life zones: Areas or bioregions where specific plant life grows; Colorado's five plant life zones are based on elevation.

native: Plants that grow naturally in a particular region and are an essential part of the landscape.

nonnative: Plant species that were transported from outside the United States and introduced here either intentionally or accidentally; also referred to as an introduced species, exotic species, or alien species.

noxious weed: A nonnative species that aggressively invades an area and causes agricultural or environmental damage. It is listed by a federal, state, county, or local agency for eradication or management.

organic fertilizers: Fertilizers derived from natural sources such as manure.

perennial: Plants that grow through several seasons and can live for many years.

microclimates: A small localized climate within a larger region.

soil pH: A condition of the soil that affects plant growth; indicates the acidity or alkalinity of the soil.

soil tilth: The physical aspects of the soil that support plant growth.

water conservation: Any beneficial reduction in water losses and water usage.

weed: A plant that is invasive and alien to the surrounding ecosystem.

woody perennial: A perennial plant that develops a woody base or root system.

Xeriscape: A termed coined by Denver Water to describe a landscape designed to conserve water; *xeric* comes from the Greek word *Xeros* for "dry."

YARDX: The Yield and Reliability Demonstrated in Xeriscape; a five-year collaborative study to demonstrate the benefits of xeriscaping.

Appendix: Resources for the Colorado Gardener

The following resources were accurate when this book was written. Some Web sites or phone numbers may have changed since that time.

Colorado State University Cooperative Extension

- Index: www.ext.colostate.edu/index.html
- Horticulture information: www.ext.colostate.edu/menugard.html
- PlantTalk Colorado: www.planttalk.org; (888) 666–3063
- Colorado Master Gardener program: http://cmg.colostate.edu
- Mountain gardening: www.coopext.colostate.edu/gilpin/MG.shtml

Annuals and Perennials

- American Rose Society: www.ars.org
- *Best Perennials for the Rocky Mountains and High Plains,* by Celia Tannehill and James Klett, Colorado State University Bulletin 573A; 2002
- W.D. Holly Plant Environmental Research Center (PERC): http://lamar.colostate.edu/~percgard/
- Colorado State University Annual Trial Gardens: www.flower trials.colostate.edu
- *Growing Roses in Colorado,* Denver Rose Society: www.denver rosesociety.org
- Plant Select Demonstration Gardens: www.plantselect.org

Hardiness Zones, Site, and Growing Seasons

- CSU Cooperative Extension fact sheets:

  Flowers for Mountain Communities (7.406)

  Ground Covers for Mountain Communities (7.413)

  Native Herbaceous Perennials for Colorado Landscapes (7.242)

  Native Shrubs for Colorado Landscapes (7.422)

  Native Trees for Colorado Landscapes (7.421)

  Trees and Shrubs for Mountain Areas (7.423)

- "Hail, Hail, Hail: The Summertime Hazard of Eastern Colorado" by Nolan J. Doesken, *Colorado Climate* 17, no. 7 (April 1994), Special Feature section, accessed at http://ccc.atmos .colostate.edu/~hail/pdfs/hail%20_hazard.pdf

- Hardiness zone by zip code: www.arborday.org

- National Oceanic and Atmospheric Administration's weather service: www.weather.gov

- U.S. Department of Agriculture (USDA) Plant Hardiness Zone map: www.usna.usda.gov/Hardzone/

Insects and Diseases

- Bat Conservation International: www.batcon.org

- Bio-Integral Resource Center: www.birc.org

- Colorado Spider Survey, Denver Museum of Nature & Science: (303) 370–6442; www.dmns.org

- CSU Cooperative Extension fact sheet: *Spiders in the Home* (5.512)

- CSU Cooperative Extension Plant Diagnostic Clinic: (970) 491–6950

- National Pesticide Information Center, a cooperative program sponsored by Oregon State University and the U.S.

Environmental Protection Agency: (800) 858–7378;
www.npic.orst.edu

- *Spiders of North America: An Identification Manual,* American
  Arachnological Society: www.americanarachnology.org

Invasive Plants

- *A Guide to Invasive Ornamental Weeds in Colorado,* Colorado Big
  Country Resource Conservation & Development, Inc.: (970)
  945–5494, ext. 4
- Colorado Weed Management Association: (970) 887–1228;
  www.cwma.org
- Colorado's A, B, and C noxious weed lists:
  www.ag.state.co.us/csd/weeds/statutes/weedrules.pdf
- Colorado's Noxious Weed Program, Colorado Department of
  Agriculture: www.ag.state.co.us

Lawn

- Drought-tolerant turfgrasses: High Country Gardens;
  www.highcountrygardens.com
- Irrigation schedule: www.watersaver.org
- How to use an evapotranspiration controller with a sprinkler
  system: www.coloradoet.org

Soil and Soil Testing

- CSU Cooperative Extension fact sheet: *Estimating Soil Texture:
  Sandy, Loamy or Clayey?* (7.723)
- CSU's Soil, Water and Plant Testing Laboratory: (970)
  491–5061
- Denver Urban Gardens: (303) 292–9900; www.dug.org

Trees and Shrubs

- Colorado Tree Coalition: www.coloradotrees.org
- CSU Cooperative Extension fact sheet: *The Science of Planting Trees* (7.833)
- Denver Digs Trees: www.theparkpeople.org
- International Society of Arboriculture: www.isa-arbor.com
- *Save Our Shade: A Guide to Tree Care in Dry Climates:* www.watersaver.org
- Tree Care Industry Association: www.natlarb.com

Vegetables

- CSU Cooperative Extension fact sheets

  Vegetable Garden Hints (7.848)

  Vegetable Planting Guide (7.850)

Water

- Colorado Department of Public Health and Environment: www.cdphe.state.co.us/cdphehom.asp
- Colorado Division of Water Resources, Office of the State Engineer: http://water.state.co.us/groundwater/groundwater.asp
- CSU Cooperative Extension fact sheet: *Graywater Reuse and Rainwater Harvesting* (6.702)
- Denver Water: (303) 628–6000; www.denverwater.org
- Drought Monitor: http://drought.unl.edu/dm
- Plant Select Demonstration Gardens: www.plantselect.org
- Southeastern Colorado Water Conservancy District: www.secwcd.org (select "Xeriscape")

- Utility Notification Center of Colorado: (800) 922–1987; www.uncc2.org
- Watering information and a customized irrigation run schedule: www.watersaver.org
- Xeriscape Colorado: www.xeriscape.org
- Yield and Reliability Demonstrated in Xeriscape (YARDX) project: www.coloradowaterwise.org/yrdx.htm

Index

A

annuals
    care, 79
    containers, 79–82
    favorites, 77
    new introductions, 72–73
    preparing and planting, 78
    requirements, 73–74
    uses, 74–76
ants, 154–55

B

bees, 97–98
beneficial insects, 153–54, 156–57
biennials, 82–84

C

children's gardening, 69–70
Colorado's life zones, 23–25
compost, 12–14
compost tea, 59
container gardening, 79–82
cover crops, 14–15
Cranshaw, Whitney, 154–55
Creasy, Rosalind, 69
Cushing, Paula, 155–56, 157

D

disease, 66–67. *See also* integrated pest management

E

elevation and plant performance, 23–25
Elliott, Judy, 13, 14
extending the growing season, 68, 70

F

fertilizer, 9–11, 79
frost-free days, 30–31

G

gray water, 37

H

hail, 32–33
hardiness zones, 18–20
hellstrip planting, 22
herbs, 67–68
Higgins, Kris, 80
Hinkemeyer, Joan, 53–55
hydro zones, 45

I

integrated pest management
    common pests, 149
    plant problems, 150–53
    practices, 146–48
invasive plants
    defined, 130–31

invasive ornamentals, 137–38
key issues, 134–35
noxious weed list, 139–42
solutions, 136–37
irrigation, 42–43, 58–59, 121–24
schedule, 124

K

Kastler, Carole, 86
Kirby, Mary, 93–94

L

Lane, Eric, 134–37, 139
Langford, Dale, 118
lawn. *See* turfgrass
life zones, 23–25

M

MacLeod, Christina, 17, 132–33
microclimates
defined, 20–21
planting, 22
moon garden, 75
mountain gardening, 26–27
mountain pine beetle, 151
mulch, 15–16, 46, 64

N

native plants, 22–23, 92, 138

O

Ogden, Lauren Springer, 94–96

P

perennials
bloom times, 91
high-altitude, 88
planting, 94–96
requirements, 87–89
selecting, 89–92
uses, 86–87
pesticides, 157–58
pH, 7–8
Plant Select program, 45, 90, 163
Potts, Laurel, 26–27
precipitation, 29–30, 34–35
public gardens, 159–64

R

rabbits, 158
rainwater harvesting, 36–37
roses, 92–94

S

seed balls, 63
Shonle, Irene, 26–27
shrubs
high-altitude, 113
maintaining, 110–12
native shrubs, 113
planning, 109–10
planting, 110

subshrubs, 109
xeric shrubs, 111
Skogerboe, Scott, 103, 111
soil
  amendments, 11–12
  Colorado soils, 3
  pH, 7–8
  samples, 8–9
  testing, 6–7
  texture, 4–5
  tilth, 3
spiders, 155–56, 157
starting seeds, 60–61, 63,
  95–96
  germination test, 62
Swift, Curtis E., 5

T

tomato growing, 65–67
trees
  evergreen trees, 108
  fruit trees, 105
  maintaining, 105–7
  planning, 100–103
  planting, 104
  preventing injury to, 107
  xeric trees, 103
turfgrass
  compaction, 120
  growing, 116–20
  irrigation, 121–24
  mowing, 120
  pests and diseases, 127–28
  problems, 125–27

renovation, 124–25
selecting, 115–16

U

USDA Hardiness Zones, 18–20

V

vegetable gardening
  designing the space, 55–56
  irrigating, 58–59
  planning, 51–55
  planting, 62–64
  preparing, 59–61

W

waffle gardens, 55
water, 34–47. *See also* irrigation
  gray water, 37
  use rules, 36–37
weather, 28–29, 32–33
weeds, 126–27. *See also* invasive plants

X

xeriscaping
  defined, 37
  plants, 44–45, 89, 92, 103, 111
  seven steps, 39–47

About the Author

Jodi Torpey is a Denver-based garden writer and nonfiction author. Her articles have appeared in *Horticulture* and *American Gardener* magazines, the *Denver Post*, and many other regional and local publications. She is a member of the Garden Writers Association and the Colorado Authors' League. As a Colorado native and a master gardener, she has special interests in gardening in a semiarid climate, creating backyard habitats, and gardening with her dog, Rufus T. Smudge.